# Vintage Andhra Recipes



Sakāl Publications

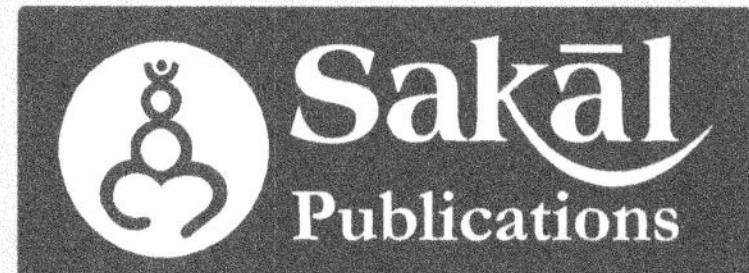

Vintage Andhra Recipes
© Vijaya Lakshmi Kalakota, 2022

First Edition:
June 2022

Concept & Author
Vijaya Lakshmi Kalakota

Designing:
Nagaraju Koppineni

Published and Printed by:
Sakal Media Pvt. Ltd.
595, Budhwar Peth,
Pune - 411 002

ISBN  978-93-89834-79-6

Enquiry Contact:
020-2440 5678 / 88888 49050
sakalprakashan@esakal.com



Images credit:
First cover page background image: https://depositphotos.com/70171233/stock-photo-herbs-and-spices-background.html
Last cover page background image: https://in.pinterest.com/pin/510947520210442018/
All images and some benefits of vegetables in this book have been collected from www.google.com; pixabay.com/users/publicdomainpictures-14/; unsplash. com/@ mockupgraphics; creativecommons.org; www.flickr.com; www.freepik.com; commons .wikimedia.org; www.tripadvisor.co.nz; www.blendwithspices .com: freepngimg.com; www.1zoom.me, istockphoto .com/ subodhsatha and some cooking websites.

Images are for representation purposes only. The recipes may vary from the images.

# Health is Wealth

We do not come across any person who does not know the saying "Health is Wealth". This is applicable to persons of all ages, languages and regions. Hence everyone must follow this golden rule of treating their health as wealth, to the extent possible, depending on their lifestyle. We can achieve anything which is lacking in our life through our efforts, but once we fall ill, we have to face innumerable types of difficulties and hardships. Health mainly depends on our food and other habits. In our country, every region has its own food habits depending upon the vegetables and fruits available in that particular region. People of different regions have different habits. The traditions and habits of South India are liked by people from all over India. The very fact that people who have settled in other countries, as also natives of those countries, like our food, is exhibited through cultivation of our food items, spices, vegetables and fruits in those countries. Every year we have been exporting these food items and day by day there is gradual increase in our exports of these items. Keeping in mind all these things, it is pertinent that, our traditional food preparations and recipes must be introduced to our future generations. This book is a compilation of simple traditional recipes without too many spices, cooked in a traditional way to preserve the natural taste. Most of us know about these recipes. However, this book would be of immense use and helpful to the newly married couples of this generation. I hope that they will learn a lot from this book.

Unlike in the olden days, today's children have no time to learn cooking and household duties from their mothers, since they are busy with their studies, and thereafter with their jobs. On getting married many such people struggle a lot, since they could not learn cooking. This book will be of immense help to such newly married people. The language used in this book is easy and can be understood by all. Following the valuable advice of doctors that we should consume as little spices as possible, I hope you will maintain good health by preparing dishes using the recipes compiled here.

— Vijayalakshmi Kalakota

| | | | |
|---|---|---|---|
| Dry Red Chilly | 2 | Toor Dal (split black gram) | ½ spoon |
| Cumin Seeds | ½ spoon | Mustard seeds | ½ spoon |
| Curry leaves | 5 to 6 | Oil | 1 spoon |

For Tamarind based items – use fenugreek seeds ½ spoon and for garnishing coriander leaves.

## Powders for some curries...

| | |
|---|---|
| Bengal gram | ¼ kg |
| Red gram | ¼ kg |
| Sesame seeds | ¼ kg |
| Drumstick leaves dry | ¼ kg |
| Pudina dry (to make powder) | ¼ kg |
| Curry leaves | ¼ kg (dry) |
| Coriander dry | ¼ kg |

Fry all the items and make powders separately and keep them in separate glass bottles, you can use them in curries. Fry them on slow fire lightly. These powders are used in whatever curry we plan to make.

### CORIANDER

Fresh coriander is a flat leaf with a sweet scented aroma and is a must in Indian cooking. It is also used as an ingredient and garnish for curries, salads and chutneys.

### BASIL

Basil is from the Tulasi plant. People call this plant as "King of Herbs".

### CURRY LEAVES

Curry leaf, an aromatic herb is popular in India. The leaves have anti-bacterial properties and are used in all curries. It is also used as a natural pesticide.

### BAY LEAF

The Bay leaf is an aromatic dried green leaf of an ever green tree. It has a strong flavour. The flavour increases with cooking time.

### FENUGREEK LEAVES

The slight bitterness gives it unique flavour. These leaves are used commonly in curries, pulav and paratha. Dried leaves are called Kasoori methi, dried leaves are stronger and therefore be used sparingly. Fenugreek leaves have been used as food and medicine and are beneficial for the treatment of indigestion and flatulence etc.

### MINT

Mint is a popular herb used mostly in Indian foods. Mint is a must in the dishes like biryani and non-veg dishes. It has many medicinal properties and is used in the treatment of many digestive, respiratory, oral and skin disorders.

# GENERAL GUIDELINES

The natural taste, flavor and color of your food is enhanced when you avoid adding food color and artificial preservatives.

Cook food on a medium or low flame to preserve the nutrients and maintain the taste.

Cutting vegetables is a skill to be acquired. Vegetables should be always cut into even pieces to ensure uniform cooking and to enhance the final appearance of the cooked food.

Asafoetida can be optionally added to the seasoning for most of the curries and chutneys as it will enhance the flavor and is good for digestion.

# Vintage
## Andhra Recipes

## SEASONING

For all curries and chutneys with cumin seeds and mustard seeds add ½ spoon mint powder, ½ spoon split bengal gram, ¼ spoon split black gram, red chilli pieces 1 no., curry leaves.

For sour curries add fenugreek powder ¼ spoon and curry leaves.

For non-veg items add 1 spoon kasuri methi.

The times given are an approximate guide only. Preparation times differ according to the techniques used by different people and the cooking times may also vary from those given. Optional ingredients, variations or serving suggestions have not been included in the time calculations.

Recipes using raw or very lightly cooked eggs should be avoided by infants, the elderly, pregnant women, convalescents and anyone suffering from an illness. Pregnant and breast feeding women are advised to avoid eating peanuts and peanut products. Suffers from nut allergies should be aware that some of the ready-made ingredients used in the recipes in this book may contain nuts. Always check the packaging before use.

# CONTENT

# SOUPS

# Carrot Soup

**Ingredients**

| | |
|---|---|
| Peeled and grated Carrots | 2 nos. |
| Finely chopped Cabbage | 1 full cup |
| Cream | 1 tsp |
| Butter | a little bit |
| Salt | to taste |
| Black pepper powder | 1/4th spoon |
| Beaten / whipped cream | 3 tsp |
| Mint leaves | 1 tsp |

**Process of preparation**

Reserve 1/4th of the carrot and cabbage and cook the remaining in a pressure cooker with a little water for two whistles. Let it cool and blend and strain the mixture. Add the reserved carrot and cabbage pieces, salt, cream, pepper powder, butter and mint leaves. Stir and serve hot.

# Ash Gourd Soup

**Ingredients**

| | |
|---|---|
| Chopped Ash gourd | 1/4th cup |
| Chopped baby onion | 1/4th cup |
| Garlic | 2 pods |
| Salt | to taste |
| Black Pepper Powder | to taste |
| Boiled and cooled milk | 1 cup |
| Cooking oil | 1 tsp |

**Process of preparation**

Saute Ash gourd pieces in oil. Add chopped baby onion and crushed garlic and fry for some time. Add salt, black pepper powder to it and pour 2 cups of water and bring to a boil. Finally add boiled and cooled milk and garnish with coriander leaves.

# Lentil Soup

**Ingredients**

| | |
|---|---|
| Onion | 1 no. |
| Olive Oil | 1/4th cup |
| Carrots | 2 nos. |
| Coriander Leaves | a little |
| Garlic Pods | 2 nos. |
| Dried basil leaves | 1 tsp |
| Bay leaf | 1 no. |
| Tomato (chopped) | 1 full cup |
| Lentils | 2 full cups |
| Water | 8 full cups |
| Spinach | ½ cup |
| Vinegar | 2 tsp |
| Salt | to taste |
| Black pepper powder | 1/4th spoon |

**Process of preparation**

Heat olive oil. Add onions, peeled and chopped garlic, carrots , tomatoes and saute. Add lentils, water and boil. Once the lentils are done, reduce flame and simmer for ½ an hour. Finally add chopped spinach, coriander, vinegar, salt, pepper and bring to a boil. It is very delicious while hot.

# Spinach Soup

**Ingredients**

| | |
|---|---|
| Green Gram | 1 tsp |
| Spinach (Chopped) | 200 gms |
| Carrots (chopped) | 100 gms |
| Radish (chopped) | 100 gms |
| Paneer (chopped) | 100 gms |
| Coconut milk | ½ cup |
| Coriander leaves (chopped) | as required |
| Amaranthus leaves chopped | ½ cup |
| Tomatoes chopped | 3 nos |
| Garam Masala Powder | ½ tsp |
| Butter | 1 tsp |
| Black Pepper Powder | little bit |
| Salt | to taste |
| Mint leaves | 10 leaves |

**Process of preparation**

Melt butter in a pressure cooker, add onion, chopped ginger and fry. Then add the green gram, chopped tomato and greens. Add water and pressure cook for ten minutes. Cool and blend the mixture. Add paneer cubes, garam masala powder and coconut milk and simmer for one minute. Serve hot.

# Garlic Vegetable Soup

**Ingredients**

| | |
|---|---|
| Finely chopped vegetables (Carrot, French beans, Cauliflower, Peanuts, Baby Corn) | 2 cups |
| Garlic Pods (peeled and crushed) | 1 tsp |
| Chopped onion pieces | ½ cup |
| Oats | 1/4th cup |
| Oil | 2 spoons full |
| Salt | to taste |
| Black pepper powder | 1/4th spoon |
| Coriander | 1/4th of a cup |
| Water | 3 cups |

**Process of preparation**

Heat oil. Add chopped garlic and chopped onion and saute. Add Vegetables and fry for some more time. Pour 3 cups of water, add salt, and pepper powder. Bring it to boil and reduce flame. Keep cooking till the vegetables become soft. Then add the oats and simmer for another 5 minutes .Switch off the stove and garnish with chopped coriander leaves. Serve hot.

# Lime-Coriander Soup

**Ingredients**

| | |
|---|---|
| Corn flour | 3 tsp |
| Ginger | 2 inches |
| Garlic | 2 pods |
| Lime | 1 No. |
| Coriander (chopped) | 1 Tsp |
| Water | 1/4th liter |
| Salt | to taste |
| Black Pepper Powder | ½ tsp |

**Process of preparation**

Heat water in a pan, add garlic, ginger and chopped coriander and boil. Dissolve corn flour in cold water without lumps and add to the boiling mixture stirring all the time. Simmer for 10 minutes and add salt, pepper powder and lime juice and remove from stove. This soup should be served while it is hot.

# Tomato Soup

**Ingredients**

| | | | |
|---|---|---|---|
| Tomatoes | 4 nos. (cut into pieces) | Onions | 1 no. (sliced) |
| Carrots | 1 no. (grated) | Beetroot | 1 no. (for colour) |
| Garlic | 4 pods (crushed) | Pepper | 5 nos. (or ½ tsp powder) |
| Ghee/Oil | 1 Tsp. | Water | 500 ml. |
| Salt | To taste | Coriander | ½ cup |
| Mint leaves (chopped) | ½ cup | | |

**Process of preparation**

Keep a thick vessel on stove and add ghee. After 2 minutes add all the ingredients and saute for 5 minutes let it become soft. Put the paste in mixture grinder, add 500 ml and simmer for 5 minutes. Take out from the stove, drain the soup add bread sticks. Garnish with coriander. Soup will be very tasty and colourful.

Snacks

# Mirchi Bajji (Green Chilly Fritters)

**Ingredients**

| | | | |
|---|---|---|---|
| Long thick green chillies | 10-12 | | |
| Coriander leaves | 1 tsp | Cooking oil | as required |
| Mint leaves | 1 tsp | Spices for stuffing chillies | |
| Salt | to taste | Chilly powder | 1 tsp |
| Chat masala | 1 tsp | Split green gram | 1 cup |
| Chilly flakes | 1 tsp | Cumin powder | 1 tsp |
| Cooking oil | 1 tsp | Dry mango powder | ½ tsp |
| Baking soda | a pinch | Garam masala powder | ½ tsp |

**For batter**

| | |
|---|---|
| Bengal gram flour | 2 cups |
| Salt | to taste |
| Chilly powder | to taste |

**Process of preparation**

Mix the spices mentioned above for stuffing the Chillies and set aside. Now slit the Chillies vertically, remove the seeds, and stuff the spices mixture and set aside. In another bowl add bengal gram flour, chilly powder, water and salt and prepare a batter of dipping consistency.

Heat oil in a pan. Dip the Chillies in the Bengal gram dough and  deep fry in hot oil till golden brown.

# Arati Bajji

**Ingredients**

| | |
|---|---|
| Raw Banana (Cut in thin slices) | 1 no. |
| Bengal gram flour | 1 cup |
| Rice flour | ½ cup |
| Cumin seeds | a little bit |
| Chilly powder | 1 tsp |
| Baking soda | ½ tsp |

**Process of preparation**

Prepare dough with bengal gram flour, rice flour, cumin seeds, salt, chilly powder and baking soda along with sufficient water to prepare a batter of dipping consistency. Dip the sliced banana pieces in batter and deep fry till golden brown. Serve hot with either ginger chutney or tomato chutney as an evening snack.

# Snack with Lentils

**Ingredients**

| | |
|---|---|
| Green gram | 1 cup |
| Finely chopped Curry leaves | 1 spoon full |
| Black gram | 1/4th cup |
| Chilly Powder | 1 t spoon |
| Split Bengal gram | 1 cup |
| Coriander leaves | 1 little bit |
| Green chillies paste | 1/4th cup |
| Cooking oil | as necessary |
| Ginger pieces | 1 t spoon |
| Salt | to taste |

**Process of preparation:** Soak green gram, Bengal gram and Black Gram separately in water for 2hrs grind them separately to a paste. Mix the three pastes with chillis, ginger pieces, curry leaves and make a dough. Make small balls of the dough and deep fry in hot oil till golden brown in color. Remove from the pan and cut each ball into 2 pieces and fry the pieces once again for 2 minutes .Remove from the pan. Drain excess oil and serve the tasty and crispy snack along with tamarind chutney.

# Uppu Chekkalu

**Ingredients**

| | |
|---|---|
| Rice flour | 500 gms |
| Split Bengal gram | little bit |
| Soaked green gram | 100 gms |
| Red chilly powder | 1 tb spoon |
| Salt | to taste |
| Cooking oil | 500 ml |

**Process of preparation**

Take a big bowl, mix rice flour, soaked green gram, bengal gram ,salt, red chilly powder and 50gm of warm Oil with water to make dough like Chapathi dough. Let it marinate for a while. Heat oil for deep frying. Make small lime sized balls of the dough and flatten the balls with hands, and drop the flattened dough into the hot oil for deep frying the color turns brownish and become crisp. This crisp and tasty snack can be stored for a week or up to 10 days and relished.

# Chekodi

**Ingredients**

| | |
|---|---|
| Rice flour | 500gms |
| Cooking oil | 500 ml |
| Soaked green gram | 100gms |
| Butter | Little bit |
| Red Chilly powder | to taste |
| Salt | to taste |

**Process of preparation**

Soak Green Gram in water for a few hours. Take a tray or a bowl, mix rice flour, soaked Green Gram, dry chilly powder, salt and little quantity of butter (so as to make the snack, crispy/s and make a dough Chapathi dough). Let it marinate for a while. Next, make small balls of the dough spread the dough like a thin ring or a circular shape out of it. Drop slowly in the hot oil and deep fry till the rings turn brown and crisp. This tasty snack can be stored for 8-10 days.

# Strings of Split Bengal Gram

**Ingredients**

| | |
|---|---|
| Bengal gram flour | 3 cups |
| Baking soda | little bit |
| Rice flour | ¼ the cup |
| Salt | to taste |
| Cumin powder | 2 tspoons |
| Ajwain | 3 tspoons |
| Chilly powder | 3 tspoons |
| Cooking oil | as required |

**Process of preparation**

Heat one table spoon oil and mix with Bengal Gram and rice flour. Add Ajwain / Vaamu powder, Salt, Cumin powder and baking soda. Add some water and mix it with the ingredients so as to make a dough. Take a frying pan, pour oil in it, and heat it up. Take a SEV press and add balls of dough and press into hot oil. Fry till brown and crisp. Store in air tight containers.

# Jantikalu

**Ingredients**

| | |
|---|---|
| Rice Flour | 4 cups |
| Bengal gram flour | 1 cup |
| Red Chilly powder | 2 tspoons |
| Cumin powder | 2 tspoons |
| Ajwain | 2 tspoons |
| Baking Soda | little bit |
| Cooking oil | as required |

**Process of preparation**

Take a Bowl and mix the split Bengal Gram and Rice flour, Chilly powder, Cumin powder, Ajwain powder, salt and baking soda and add water and make a dough. Add one table spoonful of oil to make the snack crisp. Heat oil and press dough into the hot oil using the appropriate disc in sev press. Fry till golden brown and store in airtight container.

# Pakoda

**Ingredients**

| | |
|---|---|
| Potatoes | 1 or 2 |
| Chilli powder | to taste |
| Pomegranate seeds powder | 1 tsp |
| Ajwain / Vaamu | 1 tsp |
| Cauliflower | 100 gms |
| Turmeric | to taste |
| Baking soda | Pinch |
| Coriander | to taste |
| Bengal gram flour | l cup |
| Cumin seeds | 1 tsp |
| Onions | 2 nos. |
| Cooking oil | to taste |
| Salt | to taste |
| Green chillis | 5-6 nos |
| Spinach | 1 or 2 |

**Process of preparation**

Chop all vegetables in required size, add these vegetable pieces to the Bengal gram flour with Ajwain, Baking soda, Salt, Chilly powder, Turmeric and Pomegranate seeds powder and a little water to make a stiff dough and keep aside. Heat oil and add small lumps of the dough into the hot oil and fry it till the pakodas becomes crisp and brownish. Serve the pakodas hot along with fried Green Chillis. This is a very tasty evening snack.

# Khara Boondi

**Ingredients**

| | |
|---|---|
| Bengal Gram Flour (Besan) | 4 cups |
| Red chilly powder | 1 tspoon |
| Rice Flour | 2 cups |
| Curry leaves | a few leaves |
| Cooking Oil | 500 gms |
| Baking soda | little bit |
| Cumin Powder (Dry Roast & Grind) | 1 tsp |
| Cashew nuts | as desired |
| Salt | to taste |

**Process of preparation**

Mix Bengal Gram Flour, Rice Flour and a pinch of Baking soda and add water sufficient to make a runny dough which can easily flow into the frying pan when dropped into the Oil with the Boondi Maker. Pour Oil in the wide pan, allow it to heat sufficiently till it is ready for deep frying. Now take the dough on to the Boondi maker and see that the droplets of the dough freely fall into the hot Oil, and Boondi is deep fried. It should be deep fried till it acquires reddish color and is crisp. Next step is to deep fry the Curry Leaves till the leaves also become crisp or crunchy. Add these crunchy Curry Leaves along with Chilly Powder, Salt and Cumin Powder (Quantity of each depending on the requirement of your taste) and mix this mixture in the hot Boondi thoroughly. Once the boondi cools the spices will not be absorbed into the Boondi. Hence, in every round, when you deep fry Boondi and place it in a big bowl or tray, you must immediately mix the Chilly Powder, Cumin Powder and Crunchy Curry Leaves while it is hot so as to make Boondi spicy and tasty. Fried Cashew nuts are added to the spiced Boondi. This is a ready to eat, tasty snack and relished by one and all irrespective of age.

# Blackgram Snacks
## (Minapa Garelu/Vadalu)

**Ingredients**

| | |
|---|---|
| Split Black Gram | 250 gms |
| Curry leaves | 5 twigs |
| Salt | to taste |
| Onion | 2 nos. |
| Cooking Oil | 250 gms |
| Ginger (chopped) | 1 inch |
| Cumin | 1 tsp |
| Coriander leaves | few twigs |
| Green Chillis | 8 Nos |

**Process of preparation**

Soak split Black Gram for three hours in water and grind in a mixer, without adding any water. Add green Chillis, Onions, Ginger pieces, Cumin seeds, Curry leaves and chopped Coriander and blend it thoroughly and keep aside. Take a frying pan, heat oil in it. Drop flattened discs of dough into the oil (with a hole in between if desired) and deep fry till golden brown colour. Serve Garelu with Tomato Chutney or Coconut Chutney. In some areas people eat these snacks along with mutton or Chicken Curry. In Telugu there is a saying which means that, if you want to eat something tasty or delicious- then it is garelu / vadas only and if you have to listen any story it is the Mahabharat. Such is the popularity of this snack.

# Spicy Snacks Vadas
## (Masala Garelu / Vadalu)

**Ingredients**

| | |
|---|---|
| Raw Split Bengal Gram | 50 gms |
| Cooking oil | 250 gms |
| Onions | 2 nos |
| Curry leaves | few twigs |
| Split Black Gram | 100 gms |
| Green chillis | 8 nos. |
| Ginger | 1 inch long |
| Coriander leaves | few twigs |
| Split Green Gram | 50 gms |
| Rice | 1 tsp |
| Cumin | 1 tsp |

**Process of preparation**

Take a bowl, pour some water in it, mix all the lentils together and soak in the water for 3-4 hours. Grind soaked lentils without water, and add salt, add chopped Onion, Green Chillis, Ginger, Cumin, Curry Leaves and chopped Coriander and blend the mixture into a dough. Take a piece of muslin cloth , place lime sized balls of the dough and press or flatten into thin discs and set aside. Heat oil and deep fry the discs one by one till the vadas / Garelu turn into golden brown color.

These vadas / garelu are very tasty and do not require any chutney for accompaniment. We can also mix cashew pieces in the dough and prepare vadas.

# Okra Pakodi

**Ingredients**

| | | | |
|---|---|---|---|
| Okra | ½ kg | Bengal Gram powder | 150 gms |
| Salt | to taste | Cooking oil | sufficient for frying |
| Corn flour | 50 gms | Chaat masala powder | 2 tsps |
| Lime | 1 No. | | |

**Process of preparation**

First of all, clean Okra in water, dry, remove foot stock of each Okra and open it vertically. Spread all the cut okra pieces in a wide tray and allow the okra to dry for 2-3 hours. Roll the dried okra in corn flour so that all the seeds within the okra are removed and settle down in the bottom of the tray. Remove these seeds and let the okra dry for one more hour.

In another bowl, take Bengal gram flour, salt, chilli powder, Turmeric, Chaat masala powder, Coriander leaves (finely chopped), dried Okra and water and blend to a soft dough. Heat oil. Add Okra one at a time from the dough and deep fry like pakodis till it becomes crisp, garnish with chopped coriander leaves.

# Paneer Pakoda

**Ingredients**

| | | | |
|---|---|---|---|
| Bengal gram flour | 3 cups | Water | sufficient for mixing |
| Garam Masala | ½ tsp | Cooking oil | 2 tsp |
| Paneer | 400 gms | Baking soda | one pinch |
| Dried Mango Powder | ½ tsp | Red chilli powder | 1 tsp |
| Mint leaves (chopped) | ½ cup | | |

**Process of preparation**

Cut paneer into small pieces and add all ingredients except Bengal gram flour to paneer and blend them. Keep it aside for 5 minutes. Dip Paneer mixture into the Bengal Gram flour mixed with water and deep fry. This snack is very tasty when eaten along with Chilly sauce or Groundnut Chutney.

# Corn Cutlet

**Ingredients**

| | | | |
|---|---|---|---|
| Corn | 1 cup | Green Chillis | 4 nos |
| Bread Crumbs | 2 cups | Onion | 2 nos |
| Garlic (peeled) | 1 tsp | Small Potatoes | 2 nos |
| Ginger | 1 tsp | Salt | to taste |
| Chilly Flakes | 2 tsps | Butter | 1 tsp |
| Black Pepper Powder | ½ tspoon | Coriander leaves | as required |
| Red Chilly Powder | 1 tspoon | Cooking oil | as required |
| Mixed Herbs | 1 tspoon | Eggs (for coating) | 2 nos |

**Process of preparation**

Boil Potatoes and peel the skin. Heat 2tsps of oil and butter and add chopped Ginger-Garlic, Green Chillis and Onion and sauté. Mash the peeled and boiled Potatoes and add to the pan along with herbs, Chilly Flakes, Chilly Powder, Coriander leaves (Chopped) and sauté for 5mins. Place the mixture in the bowl after it cools and then add bread crumbs. Shape small round balls of the mixture with your hands and press it into the shape of a cutlet, dip in the egg whites and drop each cutlet separately in hot oil for deep frying. This snack is a tasty one and should be dipped in either Chutney or Sauce and relished.

# Drumstick Cutlets

**Ingredients**

| | |
|---|---|
| Drumstick pieces | 450 gms |
| Butter | 50 gms |
| Onion (chopped) | 2 tbsp |
| Garlic | to taste |
| Garlic paste - | 1 tsp |
| Rice powder | 2 tsp |
| Cooking oil | Enough for frying |
| Cashew nuts | a few |
| Black pepper Powder | 1 tsp |
| Egg (white) | 1 no |
| Curry leaves | As required |
| Onion pieces | a few |
| Lime (squeezed) | 2 nos |
| Potato (boiled & mashed) | 2nos |
| Cumin powder | ½ tsp |

**Process of preparation**

Heat 2 tbsp of oil, sauté chopped onion, green chillies, mashed potatoes, drumstick pulp, cumin seeds. Thereafter, add black pepper powder, salt, lime juice, rice powder to the mixture and stir properly. Now remove from the stove & after ingredients cool down, make small balls of the entire mixture. Beat one egg, separate its white portion in a small bowl and keep it aside. Dip the balls into the egg white and deep fry in the hot oil. Heat 2tsps of oil and season with chopped onion, green chillis, cashew nuts, curry leaves & pour over fried drumstick cutlets and serve.

# Mushroom Cutlets

**Ingredients**

| | |
|---|---|
| Mushroom | 200gms |
| Green Chillies | 6 nos |
| Black Pepper Powder | 1/4 t sp |
| Egg | 1 no |
| Potatoes | ½ kg |
| Coriander leaves | 1/4 cup |
| Salt | to taste |
| Bread crumbs | 100 gms |
| Onion | 2 Nos |
| Cooking oil | as required |
| Lime | 1 no. |

**Process of preparation:** Wash Mushrooms in boiling water, and cut into small pieces, also boil Potatoes, peel and mash them and set aside. Take a frying pan, pour some oil, heat it and put chopped onions, Green Chilly and fry a little and add mashed Potatoes later, add salt, required quantity of limejuice and stir the ingredients. Later, add chopped mushroom pieces also to it. Make small balls of the cooked stuff and press or flatten these balls in a cloth piece and keep aside. Crack the egg and separate it's white portion (from yolk) and add salt to taste, whip it and set aside. Now take mushroom balls / vadas, dip in the egg white and roll them in bread crumbs and fry till it gets red in color and becomes crunchy. We can relish these tasty mushroom vadas with tomato sauce.

Vegetable Curries

# Raw Banana

## Raw Banana Curry with Coconut

**Ingredients**

| | |
|---|---|
| Raw bananas | 2 Nos ( sliced into cubes) |
| Coconut | Fine paste to taste |
| Salt | to taste |
| Chilly Powder | To taste |
| Turmeric | 1/4 tsp |
| Cooking oil | For seasoning |
| Seasoning ingredients | Mustard & Cumin seeds |
| Curry leaves | 2 Nos |
| Coriander | Little bit |
| Green Chillies | 2 Nos (Chopped) |
| Onion | 1 No (sliced) |

**Process of preparation**

Keep the frying pan over the stove, heat the oil for a few minutes, add the seasoning  ingredients in the hot oil, wait till you hear the seeds crackling. Now, put banana pieces and onion pieces and let these pieces cook for sometime. Now add salt, chilly powder and turmeric and mix them well. Wait for 2 minutes and add finely ground coconut paste. Let the ingredients cook for a while. Then mix a little bit of zeera or cumin powder and switch off the flame. Remove the curry from the pan and transfer it in a bowl. The curry will be tasty along with rice or chapathi.

## Raw Banana / Plantain Curry

**Ingredients**

| | |
|---|---|
| Raw Banana | 2 Nos (Sliced) |
| Onion | ½ cup (sliced) |
| Green chillies | 2 Nos (cut into small size) |

<u>For Seasoning</u>

| | | | |
|---|---|---|---|
| Mustard seeds | ½ Tsp | Cumin seeds | ½ Tsp |
| Curry Leaves | 2 Sprigs | Coriander | Little bit |
| Turmeric | ¼ Tsp | Cooking Oil | 1 tsp (For Seasoning) |
| Salt | To taste | Chilly Powder | 1 tsp (or as per taste) |
| Garlic | 2 cloves | | |

**Process of preparation**

Keep the frying pan on stove, pour oil and after it heats up, put the seasoning ingredients. Let the seeds splutter in oil, then add the sliced  Raw Banana, Onion and Green Chilly. Let the ingredients cook for a while. Add Salt and Turmeric and after 2 minutes, add  mashed Garlic. Mix the Chilly powder in the cooking curry, remove the pan from the stove, sprinkle coriander over the curry, then mix it nicely before transferring the ingredients into a bowl. If interested, you can add grated coconut also. Mix it well and wait for 2 minutes before serving.

# Raw Banana Chutney

**Ingredients**

| | | | |
|---|---|---|---|
| Raw Banana | 2 Nos | Onion | ½ cup (sliced) |
| Green chillies | 5-6 (sliced) | Tamarind | Little bit (to be soaked in water) |
| Salt | to state | Cooking oil | 2 tspoons (for seasoning) |
| Onion | 1 no. (cut into pieces) | Garlic cloves | a few |

**Process of preparation**

Heat oil. Add Raw Banana Slices, sliced Green Chilly and wait till the Banana Slices cook and become soft. Blend the garlic, chilly, soaked tamarind, and curd to a coarse mixture and then add cooked banana slices, salt to taste and run the mixer for a few seconds to blend. Heat oil and add the seasoning ingredients. Let it splutter and then add sliced Onions. After 2 minutes, add the ground mixture of Bananas, stir well and transfer to a serving bowl. Garnish with chopped Coriander. This dish will be good with either rice or Chapathis.

# Bottle Gourd

## Benefits of Bottle Gourd

Bottle Gourd - Curry prepared from this vegetable is beneficial to our body in the following way:

1. It reduces body heat/temperature.
2. It enhances stamina
3. If eaten in the form of sour curry, it is more beneficial than other preparations, as it prevents constipation and dullness due to excess heat in the body.
1. More Fiber and less calories
2. Vitamin 'C', minerals, B-complex, calcium, Iron, Sodium, Potassium & Bioflavonoids.
3. 100 gm of this Gourd gives only 12 Calories
4. It reduces weight if its juice is consumed regularly
5. It has cooling effect on pulse
6. High fiber content available in this Gourd prevents constipation.
7. It prevents Insomnia or sleeplessness
8. If the juice of bottle gourd is consumed regularly, the skin becomes healthy and glows

**Precaution :** Before preparing its juice, bite a piece of the Bottle Gourd. If it is bitter, throw it away and do not mix in other Juices.

# Bottle Gourd Curry

**Ingredients**

| | | | |
|---|---|---|---|
| Bottle Gourd | 1 cup chopped into small pieces | Onion | 1 no. finely chopped |
| Green Chillies | a few chopped | Salt | to taste |
| Chilli powder | 1 tsp | Turmeric | 1/4 tsp |
| Other items | Curry leaves & coriander | Mustard | 1 tsp |
| Cumin seeds | 1 tsp | | |

**Process of preparation**

Mix the Bottle Gourd pieces with salt and keep aside. Place the frying pan on the stove, heat oil and add mustard and cumin seeds, wait till they crackle. Now add the chopped bottle gourd , onion, green chilly and allow the ingredients to cook covered for sometime. When bottle gourd is done add turmeric, chilly powder to taste. Add coriander leaves  and remove from stove.  We can also add little milk while cooking process is on and lastly coriander leaves can be sprinkled over the curry and transferred into another bowl. This is a tasty dish, which can be had with both rice and chapathis .

# Bottle Gourd-Coconut Curry

**Ingredients**

| | | | |
|---|---|---|---|
| Bottle Gourd | 2 cups | Mustard seeds | ½ Tsp |
| Grated Coconut | 2 Cups | Soaked Rice | 1 Tsp |
| Green Chillies | 3 Nos | Cumin seeds | ½ Tsp |
| Dried Red Chillies | 4 Nos | Black gram | ½ Tsp |
| Tamarind pulp | 1 Tsp | Gingelly seeds | ½ Tsp |
| Coriander seeds | 1 tsp | Turmeric powder | 1/4th Tsp |

**Process of preparation**

Dry roast Gingelly seeds, coriander seeds, curry leaves,  cumin seeds, coriander  and red chillies and grated coconut. Cool and grind these with soaked tamarind. Pour some water in a vessel, add bottle gourd pieces, green chilly pieces, turmeric and boil till they become soft.  Add ground paste  to the boiled bottle gourd  with salt and let it boil for some more time. Finally add coriander leaves, and  remove from stove.

# Bottle Gourd - Butter Milk Sour Curry

**Ingredients**

| | | | |
|---|---|---|---|
| Bottle Gourd Pieces | 2 cups | Green Chillies | 2 or 3 |
| Grated coconut | 1 cup | Coriander leaves | a few twigs |
| Cooking Oil | 1 tspoon | Red chillies | 2 nos. |
| Cumin 7 Mustard seeds | 1 tspoon | Salt | to taste |
| Carom Seeds powder | 1 tspoon | Whole Curd | 1 cup |

**Process of preparation**

Wash Bottle Gourd peel off its skin, and cut into desired sized pieces. Boil the Bottle Gourd pieces in hot water mixed with Salt. Strain the water and transfer boiled Bottle Gourd pieces into a bowl. In a mixer take grated Coconut , Dry Red Chillies and Green Chillies and grind all of these into a fine paste. Collect the paste in a bowl and add the paste to the pre-boiled Bottle Gourd pieces and cook the ingredients on slow flame. When it is properly cooked add whipped Curd and water to it and stir all ingredients and cook for a while. The tasty Bottle Gourd-Buttermilk Sour Curry is ready.

# Bottle Gourd Sour Curry

**Ingredients**

| | | | |
|---|---|---|---|
| Bottle gourd | 2 cups | Curry leaves | a few twigs |
| Onion (sliced) | 1 no. | Jaggery | Little bit |
| Cooking Oil | 1 spoon | Turmeric | 1/4 tsp |
| Green Chillies | 2 nos. | Salt | to taste |
| Coriander Leaves | a few twigs | Tamarind | Lime sized ball |

**Process of preparation**

Wash Bottle Gourd, peel and cut into small pieces. Slice Onion, chop Green Chillies and coriander leaves and set aside, crush the jaggery and keep in a small bowl. Soak Tamarind in water at least ½ an hour beforehand and squeeze it to extract its pulp / juice and keep apart.

Heat oil in a pan and then add Cumin & Mustard seeds as well as Curry leaves to it. When they crackle add sliced Onions, Green Chilly and bottle Gourd pieces, followed by Salt, Red Chilly powder, Turmeric powder and Tamarind Pulp/ Juice. Continue cooking until all the ingredients are blended well. When the bottle gourd pieces are fully cooked add crushed jaggery and stir and remove after a few minutes.

The curry made from this vegetable is very tasty and it cleanses the digestive tract along with enhancing our appetite. It is good for people with multiple ailments. If Ghee and Masalas are added, the inherent quality of Ridge Gourd of creating 'Vaata' or air/gas related problems are eliminated and those suffering from gastric problems or 'Vaata' can relish it without any side effects.

# Ridge Gourd Curry

**Ingredients**

| | | | |
|---|---|---|---|
| Ridge Gourd | 250 gms | Garlic | 4 cloves |
| Onion | 1 no. chopped | Salt | to taste |
| Green Chillis | 2 nos. | Seasoning (Mustard & Cumin) | as required |
| Turmeric | 1/4 tsp | Cooking oil | 1 tsp |
| Chilly Powder | 1 spoon | | |

**Process of preparation**

Peel and chop the Ridge Gourd.  Chop the Green Chillies. Rub some salt to the Gourd pieces as a result of which water oozes out of them.  Heat oil in a pan and add seasoning, once they crackle add turmeric. Add chopped onion  and green chilly  as well as the ridge gourd  (after squeezing the water out of them). After the ingredients are cooked properly, add crushed garlic pods along with Chilly powder, cook it on flame for a minute or so and remove from stove before garnishing it with freshly chopped coriander leaves.

This preparation is suitable for eating along with rice as well as Chapathis. You can also add a cup of milk while the ingredients are boiling but for this the garlic is not needed. If interested you can also add grated coconut (either dried or fresh) to the dish.

# Ridge Gourd Chutney

**Ingredients**

| | | | |
|---|---|---|---|
| Ridge Gourd | ¼ kg | Cumin Seeds | 1 Tsp |
| Green Chillis | 10-15 | Curry Leaves | a few |
| Tamarind | Lemon sized | Coriander Leaves | a few |
| Salt | to taste | Cooking Oil | 1 Tsp |
| Garlic | 5 pods | | |

**Process of preparation**

Remove the skin of the Ridge Gourd, cut it into pieces and set aside. Heat oil in a pan and add the pieces of Ridge Gourd, Green Chillis, and let the ingredients simmer on medium flame. Then add tamarind to this to make the ingredients softer. Cool and grind alongwith garlic, cumin seeds, curry leaves and salt. Sprinkle a little bit of chopped coriander leaves. This does not require seasoning and is a very tasty dish.

# Ridge Gourd with Lentils

**Process of preparation**

Soak a cup of either Chana dal (Bengal Gram) or Moong Dal (Green Gram) for an hour in water and pour in a strainer to strain the extra water out.  Heat oil in a pan, add mustard and cumin seeds and wait till seeds splutter. Then, add the Ridge Gourd pieces, soaked and drained lentils viz. Chana Dal or Moong Dal along with chopped onions and Green chilly , Chilly powder and turmeric powder and  add a cup of water and cook. Finally add salt and chopped coriander  and remove from flame. Now the tasty dish is ready for serving.

# Bitter Gourd

In the olden days people consumed this vegetable extensively, since this is a remedy for various diseases. The high Fiber content in it prevents constipation and it is a very good cure for diabetes.

## Bitter Gourd (Kakarakaya) Curry

### Ingredients

| | | | |
|---|---|---|---|
| Bitter Gourd | 1/4th kg | Curry leaves | 4 leaves |
| Sour Buttermilk | 1 cup | Salt | to taste |
| Tamarind | Lemon sized | Onion | 1/4 kg |
| Garlic-Chilly finely ground powder | 3 tsps | Cooking oil | 3 tbsps |
| Cumin Powder | 1 tsp | Coriander powder | 1 tsp |
| Garlic pods | 8 nos. | Jaggery | optional |

### Process of preparation

First wash the Bitter Gourd . Do not remove the foot stalk (called Todima in Telugu) of the vegetable, as if it is removed, water will enter the inside of the vegetable and will absorb extra oil while being cooked and then it will take extra time to get fried. Keep the Bitter Gourd in a thick bowl and apply Salt and Turmeric. Add Buttermilk to it and boil till the water evaporates. Take a frying pan, add 100 gms of oil to it and  heat  till  smoking. Fry 4 Bitter Gourds at a time in the oil till they turn Red/Brown and remove from the pan. Add Red Chillis, Black Gram dal, Mustard seeds, Cumin Seeds and Curry Leaves to hot oil for seasoning and then add chopped Onion. After frying the Onion, add Bitter gourd pieces and Garlic-Chilly Mixture. Mix all the ingredients nicely and garnish with chopped Coriander leaves over it before serving. If required, we can add Jaggery to it (to beat the Bitter taste of the curry.

This is a tasty curry (even without Jaggery). It is a good combination with Mudda Pappu (plain boiled dal).

# Bitter Gourd (Kakarakaya) Chutney

**Ingredients**

| | |
|---|---|
| Bitter Gourd | 1/4th kg |
| Onion Pieces | 1/4th kg |
| Tamarind | equal to 2 lemons |
| Cooking Oil | 2 tsps |
| Salt | to taste |
| Seasoning seeds | a few |
| Chilly Powder | 2 tsps |
| Coriander Leaves | a few |

**Process of preparation**

Cut the Bitter Gourd into small pieces and add Salt, Turmeric, Lime juice etc and let the pieces of Bitter Gourd soak or be steeped therein for an hour. After an hour remove the pieces of Bitter Gourd from the semi liquid mixture of Salt, Turmeric and Lime juice. Now grind coarsely in mixer and squeeze the pieces nicely and keep aside. Then add to this paste, Salt, Chilly powder, Turmeric, grind and then add Garlic and Cumin powder and mix the ingredients. Next heat some oil in a pan, add mustard and cumin seeds for seasoning and add ground paste to season it. Lastly fry the chopped Onion and add it to the Bitter Gourd paste.

# Bitter Gourd Sour Curry

**Ingredients**

| | |
|---|---|
| Bitter Gourd | 1/4 kg |
| Chilli/Mirchi powder | 3 tsps |
| Onion | 1 no. |
| Turmeric | ½ tsp |
| Green chillis | 4 nos. |
| Cooking Oil | 1 tbsp |
| Tamarind (soaked in water) | Lime sized |
| Jaggery | as necessary |
| Seasoning seeds | a few |
| (Cumin, Mustard seeds etc.) | |

**Process of preparation**

Wash and cut the bitter gourd into long pieces. Extract pulp from tamarind, add bitter gourd and chopped onion pieces to it place it in a vessel with water and allow it to boil. Add chilli powder, turmeric powder, salt and jaggery. Stir all ingredients and continue to boil. Allow it to boil till the tamarind juice condenses and becomes thick. Season finally with mustard and cumin seeds.

# Bitter Gourd (Kakarakaya) Fry

**Process of preparation**

First cut the Bitter Gourd into round pieces and add to it some Butter milk and Tamarind juice, Salt and Turmeric, cook and set it aside. Pour some cooking oil in a pan, heat up the oil and fry the Bitter Gourd pieces. In a small bowl take some oil, heat the oil, and add Cumin and Mustard to the hot oil. Then add chopped Onion, finely powdered mixture of Garlic, Cumin & Chilly and fried bitter gourd, mix it nicely. Garnish with finely chopped fresh Coriander leaves.

# Snake Gourd

1. It cures us from 3 Doshas i.e. disorders of three types in the body viz. Wind, Bile and Phlegm.

2. This vegetable if consumed acts as a Regimen Diet and helps cure fever. This vegetable also helps us improve our appetite and allows free bowel movement. It also safeguards our body by maintaining its temperature and health adjusted to all seasons, uniformly.

**Precaution:** Those who have the tendency of excessive Phlegm frequently, must consume this curry by adding mustard seed powder or spices.

## Snake Gourd + Red Gram Curry

### Ingredients

| | | | |
|---|---|---|---|
| Snake gourd pieces | 2 cups | Red Chilly Powder | 1 spoon |
| Red Gram Dal | 1 cup | Garlic pods | 5 nos. |
| Onion | 1 no. | Seeds for seasoning | as desired |
| Green Chillies | 3 nos. | Curry leaves | few |
| Turmeric | ½ spoon | Coriander - chopped | |
| | | Salt | 1 Tspoon |

### Process of preparation

Chop the Snake Gourd pieces uniformly and add salt and water to cover the pieces and boil it. Add 1 cup of Red Gram to it. Allow it to boil and then strain the water. In a pan heat oil to smoking point. Add the Cumin and Mustard Seeds to the oil for seasoning . Then add chopped onion ,chopped Green chilly and boiled snake gourd pieces, Red Gram and cook all the ingredients for sometime. Add salt, Red Chilly Powder as well as Crushed Garlic Pods and mix nicely. Cook for a few minutes before putting off the stove. Lastly Garnish the Curry with Chopped Coriander leaves and relish it.

This curry will be a good accompaniment with Chapathis as well as Rice.

## Snake Gourd Curd Chutney

### Ingredients

| | | | |
|---|---|---|---|
| Snake Gourd pieces | 2 cups | Coriander (Chopped) | a few |
| Green Chillies | 10 nos. | Salt | to taste |
| Tamarind | a little bit | Curd | 1 cup |
| Cumin Seed powder | as required | Cooking Oil | 1 spoon |
| Garlic Pods | 2-3 | Cumin & Mustard seeds | as required |
| Curry Leaves | a few | | |

### Process of preparation

First boil the Snake Gourd pieces and set aside. Heat oil to smoking point and fry the green chillies. Grind Garlic pods, Tamarind, Salt and Cumin powder in a mixer. While Grinding them together make sure you grind Garlic pods first followed by all other items since if you put them all together, the Garlic pods may not  form a smooth paste. Add this paste to the green chillies followed by snake gourd and curd. Season it with Cumin, Mustard seeds and Curry Leaves.

## Snake Gourd Curry

### Ingredients

| | | | |
|---|---|---|---|
| Snake Gourd pieces | 1/4th kg | Salt | to taste |
| Onion | 1 no. | Cumin & Mustard seeds | as required |
| Green Chillies | 2-3 | Curry Leaves | as required |
| Turmeric | 1/4th spoon | Coriander Leaves | to garnish |
| Red Chilly Powder | 1 tspoon ful | Cooking Oil | 1 spoonful |
| Garlic Pods | 4 nos. | | |

### Process of preparation

Cut the Snake Gourd into equal pieces, and rub it with  Salt. Chop Onion and Green Chillies. Place a pan over the stove, light it up and add Oil. After the oil is heated up, add Cumin & Mustard seeds and Curry Leaves for seasoning. Then add chopped gourd pieces ( after squeezing out the salt water), Onion and Green Chilly pieces, Turmeric and stir nicely and allow it to cook. After it is done, add crushed Garlic and Chilly Powder and Coriander leaves and transfer to a serving bowl.

# Ivy Gourd

This vegetable, when cooked, turns out to be tasty dish. This has a very useful characteristic of removing toxins from our body. If eaten in excess, Ivy Gourd has the tendency to cause dementia or loss of memory power.

## Ivy Gourd Fry

**Ingredients**

| | | | |
|---|---|---|---|
| Ivy Gourd | 1/4th kg | Dried Coconut (grated) | 2 spoons |
| Cooking Oil | 1 tbsp | Red Chilly Powder | ½ spoon |
| Cumin & Mustard seeds | 1 tsp each | Salt | to taste |

**Process of preparation**

Take 1/4th kg of Ivy Gourd, wash it and cut into either long or round pieces. Add required quantity of salt and rub it onto the pieces thoroughly. Take Oil in a pan, heat it till smoking point. Add Cumin & Mustard seeds and Curry Leaves. Add Ivy Gourd pieces after Squeezing water out of it, and allow it to cook for a few minutes. After cooking is done, add turmeric and chilly powder to it and stir. If desired you can also sprinkle either Bengal gram flour or Dried Coconut Powder.

## Ivy Gourd Chutney (Dondakaya Chutney)

**Ingredients**

| | | | |
|---|---|---|---|
| Ivy Gourd | 1/4th cup | Salt | to taste |
| Cooking Oil | 1 tbsp | Cumin Powder | 1 tsp |
| Cumin & Mustard | as required | Tamarind | equal to a lime |
| Garlic | 3 pods | Green chillies | 3nos |

**Process of preparation**

Wash Ivy Gourd and Green Chillies and chop both. Fry in a pan and set aside.  Add Tamarind, Salt, cumin powder, Garlic pods (After peeling off its skin and crushing or chopping) and Fried vegetables in a mixer and grind together.  Ensure that the ground mixture is coarsely ground. Season chutney with mustard and cumin seeds.

# Okra

Curry made from this vegetables is very tasty and reduces the heat and cools down the body. It is beneficial to those with excess body heat, and cures diseases like gas (vaata) and diabetes. If this vegetable is cooked along with sour butter milk, then it is extremely helpful for all types of ailments.

## Okra Curry

**Ingredients**

| | | | |
|---|---|---|---|
| Okra | 250 gms | Cooking Oil | 1 tbsp |
| Green chillies | 3 nos. | Ginger | small piece |
| Chilly powder | 1 spoonful | mustard and cumin seeds | as required |
| Salt | to taste | Coriander leaves (freshly chopped) | as required |

**Process of preparation**

Wash and dry the okra  so that the okra is not sticky. Chop okra into medium size pieces and finally chop 4 chillies and ginger. Heat  oil and mustard and cumin seeds, when they crackle, add  chopped Green Chillies and ginger. Wait for a minute and add the chopped okra and add salt, turmeric to it and fry it till its water content dries up. You can add chilly powder if necessary but only after the okra pieces become soft, if you feel the green chilly is not sufficient to give pungent or hot taste of chillies. Sprinkle chopped coriander leaves and relish this tasty dish.

## Okra (Lady's finger Sour Curry)

**Ingredients**

| | | | |
|---|---|---|---|
| Okra | ½ kg | Tamarind | 50 gms. (juice) |
| Onion | 2 nos. (sliced) | Oil for seasoning | 1 tsp |
| Green chilly | 4 nos. | Red chilly powder | 1 tbsp |
| Turmeric Powder | ¼ spoon | Oil | 1 tsp |

**Process of preparation**

Cut okra into small pieces add onion piece, green chillies, salt, chilly powder, turmeric powder, add tamarind juice, heat the bowl, keep it on low heat. Put okras with all the ingredients, after 10 minutes remove the curry and season it by add coriander leaves. Take it in serving bowl.

This vegetable is helpful for diabetes patients. It cures ill effects of 'Vaata', cold, cough, asthma besides body pains. It is good for those who have bodies with excess heat.

Dosakaya (Yellow Cucumber) Curry

### Ingredients

| | | | |
|---|---|---|---|
| Dosakaya (Yellow Cucumber) pieces | 2 cups | Garlic pods 4 nos. |
| Onion | 1 no. | Mustard and cumin seeds | as required |
| Green chillies | 2-3 | Curry leaves | as required |
| Turmeric | 1/4 tsp | Coriander leaves | little bit |
| Chilly powder | 1 tbsp | Cooking oil | 1 tbsp |
| | | Salt | 1 tsp |

### Process of preparation

Chop the Cucumber (Dosakaya), onion and three Chillies and keep aside. In a pan heat oil and add the curry leaves and add mustard and cumin seeds to it. Once the  seeds crackle, add chopped onions, chillies and cucumber pieces  mixed with salt and Chilly powder as well as turmeric powder and mix all of them. Simmer covered till the cucumber pieces cook and become tender, remove from stove and garnish with coriander.

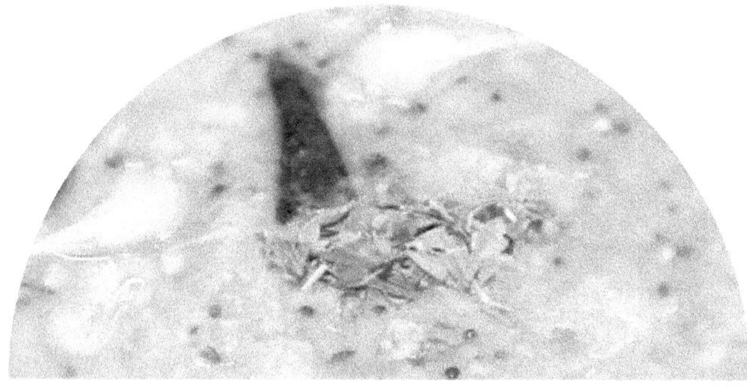

# Dosakaya (Yellow Cucumber) Dal

**Ingredients**

| | |
|---|---|
| Cucumber pieces with skin | 2 cups |
| Turmeric | 1/4 tsp |
| Red gram | 1 cup |
| Chilly powder | 1 tbsp |
| Green gram | 1 cup |
| Garlic pods | 4 nos. |
| Tamarind (soaked) | little bit |
| Salt | to taste |
| Onion | 1 no. |
| Curry leaves | sufficient |
| Coriander leaves | little bit |
| Cumin seeds | as required |
| Cooking oil | 1 tbsp |
| Mustard seeds | as required |
| Green chillies | 2 nos. |

**Process of preparation:** Boil red gram dhal in a pressure cooker. Add cucumber pieces, onion, chilly, salt, turmeric & tamarind juice to the boiled lentils. Let all the ingredients cook for 3 whistles of pressure cooker and then remove the lid and mash the dal with dhal masher. Heat oil and add mustard seeds, cumin seeds, curry leaves, once the seeds splutter add this seasoning to the cooked ingredients. Garnish with coriander leaves. This is a very tasty dal.

# Dosakaya (Yellow Cucumber) Chutney

**Process of preparation**

Roast the Cucumber on fire, peel of its skin and cut the Cucumber into big pieces. If it is not possible to roast it on fire, then apply some oil to the cucumber and place it in a cooker, let it boil, remove and then cut into pieces. Take 10 Green Chillies, Tamarind, Salt, Garlic, Cumin Powder and grind them together. Add this ground mixture to the boiled cucumber. This does not require seasoning.

# Dosakaya (Yellow Cucumber) Chutney

**Ingredients**

| | |
|---|---|
| Cucumber pieces | 2 cups |
| Salt | to taste |
| Green Chillies | 10 pieces |
| Tamarind | equal to a lime |
| Turmeric | 1/4 tsp |
| Cumin seeds powder | 1 spoonful |

**Process of preparation**

Remove the skin of the Cucumber and chop it into small pieces and take 2 cup full of these pieces add 10 Chillies and fry these in the oil. Take some tamarind, salt, garlic, cumin powder in a mixer and grind the mixture finely. Add Cucumber and Green chilly pieces to ground Ingredients. In a small pan, take some oil, heat it up and season it with cumin and mustard seeds and curry leaves and pour this seasoned oil to the ground mixture. Tasty Chutney is ready.

# Dosakaya (Yellow Cucumber) Sour Curry

**Ingredients**

| | |
|---|---|
| Cucumber with skin | 2 cups full |
| Chilly powder | 1 tsp |
| Onion | 1 no. |
| Salt | to taste |
| Tamarind | equivalent to a lime |
| Cumin & Mustard seeds | for seasoning |
| Green chillies | 3 Nos. |
| Cooking Oil | 1 tbsp |
| Turmeric powder | 1/4 tsp |
| Coriander | few strands |

**Process of preparation**

Cut the Cucumber into pieces without peeling off its skin and cook along with a little water in a pressure cooker, add chopped Onions, Green Chills, Salt, Chilly Powder, Turmeric powder to the boiling Cucumber pieces. After all ingredients are cooked and become soft, add Tamarind juice and let it again boil for some time. Then take oil in a small frying bowl, heat it up and add Cumin seeds and Mustard seeds in it and let these seeds crackle. Add this seasoning into the cooker and mix well and garnish with Coriander Leaves.

# Broad Beans

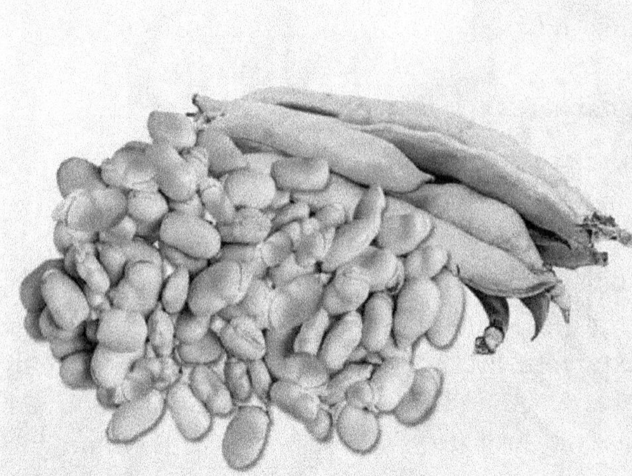

These have abundant amount of proteins which gives lot of strength to muscles and body. It has a quality of enhancing production of breast milk in lactating women. Such women should eat this curry as many times as possible instead of depending on drugs and medicines which have side effects, so as to increase their breast milk naturally and not artificially through medicines or injections etc.

Although this curry is very tasty, it creates a lot of heat in our body.

## Broad Bean Fry

**Ingredients**

| | | | |
|---|---|---|---|
| Broad Beans | 1/4th kg | Onion | 1 no |
| (cut into small pieces and boil) | | Salt | to taste |
| Chilly powder | 1 tsp | Turmeric powder | 1/4 tsp |
| Garlic | 4 pods | Mustard and Cumin seeds | 1 tsp |
| Cooking oil | 2 tbsps | | |

**Process of preparation**

Boil broad beans and keep aside. Chop one onion into pieces and set aside. Heat oil add mustard and cumin seeds and allow the seeds to crackle. Then add chopped onions and allow it to turn  brown in colour followed by boiled broad beans. Add chilly powder, salt, turmeric and mix all the ingredients well. Let the contents of the pan be uniformly cooked and soften. Lastly crush 4 pods of Garlic finely and add to the cooked beans and mix. Before removing from the pan, garnish it with freshly cut coriander leaves.

## Cluster Beans (Goru Chikkudu Kaya) Curry

**Ingredients**

| | | | |
|---|---|---|---|
| Cluster Beans | 1/4th kg | Onion | 1 no. |
| Seasoning seeds (Cumin + Mustard) | 1 spoonful | Cooking Oil | 1 tb spoon |
| Garlic-Chilly Powder | 1 tb spoon | | |
| (Mix Garlic + ½ spoon Cumin seeds + 1 tb spoon Chilly powder) | | | |

**Process of preparation**

Remove the inedible parts from the top and sides of the cluster beans and cut them into small pieces and boil. If in a pressure cooker, remove it after 1 whistle of the pressure cooker, strain the water. Heat up some oil in a small bowl, add Cumin and Mustard seeds to the heated oil, once  the seeds crackle  add chopped Onion pieces and later the boiled cluster bean pieces followed by salt,  Chilly garlic Mixture (finely ground) and mix all the ingredients till they become soft and tender. Before removing, garnish with finely chopped Coriander leaves.

If Groundnut powder or Gingelly (Til) powder is added to it in the end, then it will improve its taste.

# Drumstick

Drumstick leaves are extremely good for our health. We can prepare various types of curries with these leaves. It is also very tasty along with being beneficial for our health. The special features of these leaves are as under.

**Speciality of the Drumstick Leaves**

1. **Medicinal properties:** Nutrients are abundantly found in these leaves. But unfortunately, most people are not aware of these properties of drumstick leaves. The nutrients available in the drumstick leaves are more than other vegetables. Vitamin A content in the drumstick leaves is 4 times more abundant than in carrots. This high content of Vitamins is very beneficial to us in curing eye diseases, skin diseases, heart diseases, Diarrhea etc..

2. **Vitamin C** content in the leaves is 7 times more than oranges. These leaves are helpful in curing fever, cold, flu etc.

3. **Potassium:** These leaves give us potassium which is more than thrice potassium content in bananas. This helps in healthy and proper functioning of our Brain and its nerves and helps in being quick, active, alert as well as attentive. Three times more potassium is supplied to our brain, if we consume these leaves.

4. **Proteins:** Drumstick leaves also supply all the proteins equivalent to those contained in Eggs and hence can be supplemented along with Eggs to supply more protein to our body which means the process of health benefits due to proteins is thrice and quicker than when we consume only eggs.

5. **Building up our Body Tissues:** Unlike other vegetables these leaves have specialized quality of building up our body tissues.

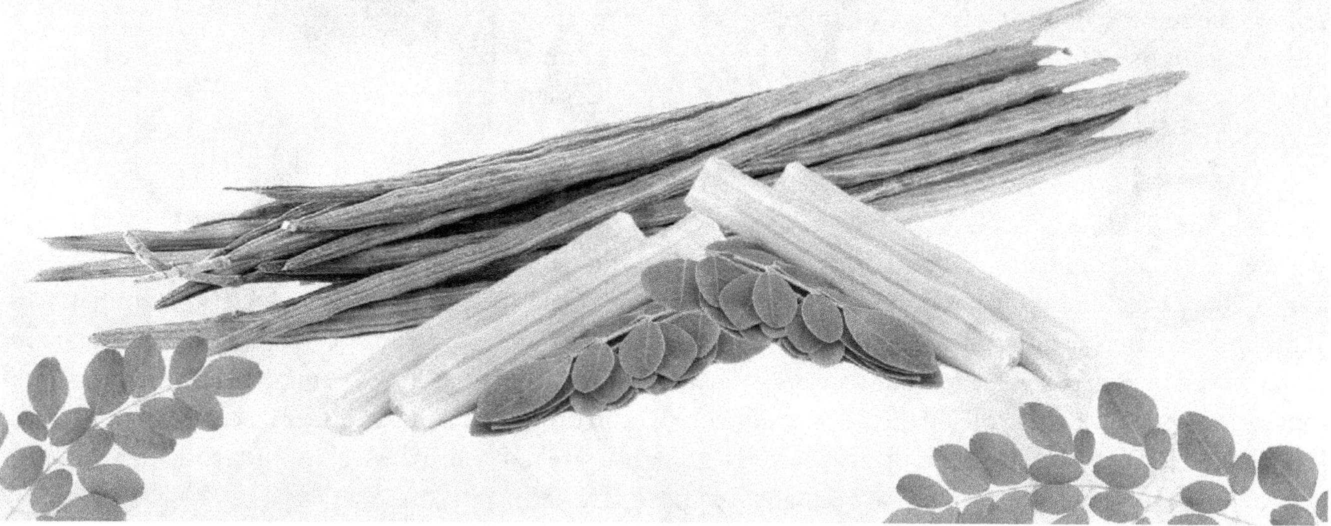

# Drumstick Curry

**Ingredients**

| | |
|---|---|
| Drumstick | 4 nos. |
| Mustard and cumin seeds | as required |
| Green Chillies | 4 nos. |
| Cooking oil | 2 tspoons |
| Onions chopped | 3 nos |
| Grated coconut | 2 tsp (optional) |
| Red Chilly powder | 1 tspoon |
| Milk | a little bit |
| Salt | to taste |

**Process of preparation**

Cut the Drumstick into two inch pieces. Heat oil add mustard and cumin seeds, once they crackle add chopped onion, Green Chillies and let them fry until the onions turn brown. Add drumstick pieces, cover and cook till the pieces become soft. Then add salt, Chilly powder and Turmeric and finally milk and mix it thoroughly. Make a paste of grated coconut in a mixer using a little bit of water and add this paste to the curry. Stir the coconut paste and wait for few minutes before removing from the stove. Add Coriander Leaves. It is very tasty with Rice.

# Drumstick Sour Curry

**Ingredients**

| | |
|---|---|
| Drumstick pieces | 2 cups |
| Red Chilly Powder | 1 tsp |
| Tamarind | as desired |
| Garlic Pods | 4 nos. |
| Onions | 1 no. |
| Cumin + Mustard seeds | as required |
| Green Chillies | 2-3 |
| Curry leaves | as required |
| Salt | as desired |
| Coriander Leaves | as required |
| Turmeric | 1/4thspoon |
| Cooking oil | 1 tbsp |

**Process of preparation**

Heat oil, add Cumin and Mustard seeds for seasoning and wait till they splutter. Add Drumstick pieces followed by Salt, Chilly Powder and Turmeric. Mix the ingredients nicely and then add the Tamarind juice prepared from the soaked Tamarind and allow all the ingredients to cook nicely. Press the Drumstick pieces with hands or spoon, if the pieces come off softer, and also if the Tamarind juice becomes thick, the curry is done. Garnish with chopped Coriander leaves and remove from stove. It tastes good with Rice.

# Drumsticks-Yellow Cucumber Sour Curry
## (Mulakkada-Dosakaya Pulusu)

**Ingredients**

| | | | | |
|---|---|---|---|---|
| Drumsticks 2 inch pieces | 2 nos. | | Salt | to taste |
| Yellow Cucumber (cut into pieces) | Cooking Oil | | 2 tsps | |
| without peeling skin) | 1 no. | | Cumin & Mustard seeds | as required |
| Onion | 1 no. | | Coriander leaves | a few twigs |
| Green Chillies | 2 nos. | | Tamarind | Equal to a Lime |
| | | | Red Chilly Powder | 1 tsp. |

**Process of preparation**

Wash and clean Drumsticks, Yellow Cucumber, Green Chillies, chop Drumsticks into pieces of 2 Inches each. Cut Yellow Cucumber (Dosakaya) in small pieces without removing its skin. Slice Onions, chop Chillies, soak Tamarind in water an hour prior to cooking. Take a thick bowl and put drumstick pieces, Yellow cucumber pieces, sliced Onion pieces, Salt, Chilly Powder, Turmeric, Tamarind pulp (by squeezing soaked Tamarind), add some water and boil all ingredients till they are fully cooked and drumstick and cucumber pieces turn soft.

Heat oil in a pan and add cumin & Mustard seeds and Curry Leaves and once the seeds splutter add to the boiled ingredients for seasoning and finally garnish the sour Curry with chopped Coriander. Have it with Rice.

# Drumstick with Coconut

**Ingredients**

| | | | |
|---|---|---|---|
| Drumsticks | 4 nos. (cut into 2 pcs. each) | Onions | 2 nos. (sliced) |
| Coconut milk | 1 cup | Green Chillies | 4 nos. (split) |
| Salt | to taste | Red chilli powder | 1 tsp. |
| Turmeric powder | ¼ spoon | Oil for seasoning | 2 tsp. |
| Coriander leaves | ¼ cup | | |

**Process of preparation**

Pour oil in a pan, keep it on low heat. Add seasoning items after the seeds splutter add drumstick pieces, onions, green chillies. Let it cook for some time, after cooking all the items add mirchi powder, turmeric, salt and pour the coconut milk. Let it cook for 5 minutes. Before taking it in a serving bowl add coriander leaves garnish. It will taste good with rice.

# Brinjal - Drumstick Sour Curry
## (Vankaya - Munagakaya Pulusu)

**Ingredients**

| | | | |
|---|---|---|---|
| Brinjal | 250 gm | Coriander leaves | Few strands |
| Drumsticks | 2 Nos. | Red Chilly powder | 1 spoon |
| Onion | 1 No (sliced) | Salt | To taste |
| Green Chillies | 2 Nos. (slit) | Turmeric powder | 1/4 tsp |
| Curry Leaves | few sprigs | Tamarind | 10 gm. |

**Process of preparation**

Wash Brinjals, Drumsticks and green Chillis in water and cut them into small pieces. Put all these items in a thick pan and add salt, chilly powder, turmeric powder and tamarind juice (Prepared one hour in advance by soaking it in water) and boil together. Heat oil in a frying pan add chopped onions, and green chilly pieces and wait till the onion turns brown. Put all the boiled ingredients in the seasoned oil and allow them to cook till the vegetables becomes soft. After cooking is done for a few minutes, garnish the sour curry, with chopped coriander before removing from stove and serve hot. This sour curry is a good accompaniment with rice.

# Beans

Beans has high Fiber Content which is very good for our health since it cleans up the intestine and facilitates free bowel movement, and it helps in preventing diabetes. Its regular use also protects us from developing cancer.

## Beans Curry

**Ingredients**

| | | | |
|---|---|---|---|
| Beans | 1/4th kg | Cooking Oil | 2 tsps |
| Onion | 2 nos. (sliced) | Garlic | 4 pods |
| Green Chillies | 2 nos. (split) | Curry leaves | a few |
| Salt | to taste | Coriander | few strands |
| Chilly Powder | 1 tsp | Turmeric | 1/4 tsp |

Seeds for Seasoning (Cumin + Mustard) – as required

**Process of preparation**

Cut the beans into small pieces after removing its midrib and fibrous part from its sides. Pressure cook the beans with sufficient water to cover the pieces till two whistles. Strain the cooked beans in a colander. Heat oil and add mustard and cumin seeds, wait till they crackle and add the cooked beans to the seasoned oil. Fry the beans for a while, and then add Salt, Chilly Powder, and crushed garlic Pods (after peeling off the skin). Mix the ingredients nicely and keep it on stove for one more minute and remove it from the stove. Garnish with coriander leaves. It is good with Rice.

## Beans Second Recipe

**Ingredients**

| | | | |
|---|---|---|---|
| Beans | 1/4th kg | Onion | 1 no. (sliced) |
| Green Chillies | 2 nos. (split) | Salt | to taste |
| Seasoning Seeds (Cumin + Mustard) | 1 tsp | Turmeric Powder | 1/4 tsp |
| Garlic | 4 pods | Coriander  chopped | 1 tbsp |
| Curry Leaves | few leaves | | |

**Process of preparation**

Remove the midrib of the Beans on both sides, cut into small pieces. Chop the Onion and Green Chillies. Boil beans in a pressure cooker. Take a pan and heat the Oil in it, add Cumin & Mustard seeds together with Curry Leaves for Seasoning to it and wait till the seeds crackle. Add Onion and Green Chillies to the seasoned oil, fry it for a while, and then add Salt (as per taste), Turmeric powder, and saute for some more time. Add Chilly Powder, peeled and crushed garlic. Garnish with finely Chopped Coriander Leaves and have it with Rice.

### Other Variations of Beans Curry

1. Soak Green Gram in water for at least one or two hours in advance, and add the same to the seasoned Beans and add a little water to it. Once the Green Gram and Beans cook properly, we can add Salt, Garlic and Chilly Powder.

2. While Seasoning the Beans, we can add half a cup of grated Coconut. This will give extra taste to the curry, and it is very good for our health.

# Brinjal

1.  This is commonly cooked curry in day to day life.
2.  The soft Brinjal removes all Tridoshas or three disorders viz. Vaata, Pitta and Kapha from our body.
3.  It is good for curing eye diseases and also gives strength to body.
4.  Brinjal should be consumed in moderation. If consumed excessively it causes pain in the bones and also damages the liver.
5.  If Brinjal Curry is eaten along with ghee or butter, its ill effects will vanish.

## Brinjal Spicy (masala) Curry

**Process of preparation**

Take round and small sized Brinjals and cut them into 4 pieces without removing the foot stalk of the brinjal, taking care to see that the pieces are not separated and are attached to each other. Fry the brinjals in oil. Take 2 spoons of Coriander seeds, Gingelly, Groundnut, Little bit of Cumin powder, few fenugreek seeds, 5 dried Red Chillis, roast all of them together and grind to a fine powder and set aside. In a small bowl collect the juice out of soaked Tamarind by squeezing well. Heat 100 gms of Oil in a pan, and then add Cumin & Mustard seeds for seasoning. To this add the roasted and ground spices mixture, tamarind juice, 2 spoons of Salt and Turmeric and mix them properly and cook. Finally add the already fried Brinjals and jaggery 2 spoons to the cooked ingredients and allow it to cook for some more time. After it is done garnish the Brinjal Curry with freshly chopped Coriander leaves and transfer it into a bowl. Another variety of this Curry is to stuff the roasted and ground spice paste into the slits made in the brinjals and fry them in Oil. This Curry is a good accompaniment to either Rice or Chapathi or Fried Rice.

## Brinjal Tomato Chutney

**Ingredients**

| | | | |
|---|---|---|---|
| Brinjals | 250 gms | Garlic | 4 pods |
| Tomatoes | 4 Nos. | Curry leaves | A few sprigs |
| Green Chillies | 50 gms | Coriander | A few twigs |
| Cooking oil | 2 tsp | Salt | to taste |
| Cumin powder | 2 tsp | Tamarind | Lime sized ball |

**Process of preparation**

Wash Brinjals and Tomatoes, cut both into pieces also chop onions and green Chillies and keep aside in different bowls. Heat oil, add chopped onion and green Chillies to it. When onion turns brown, add brinjal pieces and sliced tomatoes, followed by salt, red chilly powder & turmeric powder. Once the vegetables are cooked add tamarind and crushed garlic pods, curry leaves and cumin powder. Cool and blend all the ingredients and transfer to a bowl and garnish with chopped coriander leaves before serving.

This chutney does not need seasoning and is tasty even without seasoning.

# Brinjal - Yellow Cucumber Chutney

**Ingredients**

| | |
|---|---|
| Brinjal | 1/4 kg |
| Garlic (Skin peeled) | 6 pods |
| Yellow Cucumber | 1 no |
| Salt | to taste |
| Cooking oil | 1 tsp |
| Tamarind | Lime sized |
| Green Chillis | 50 gms |
| Cumin powder | 1 tsp |
| Curry leaves | A few sprigs |

**Process of preparation**

Cut the Brinjals, yellow cucumber and green Chillies into pieces and set aside. Soak tamarind in water. Heat oil in a pan and saute green chillies and brinjal pieces. Now grind garlic pods, cumin powder, salt, green chillies, brinjal and tamarind together. Add this ground paste of brinjal and spices etc. to the cucumber pieces (preferably skin peeled off) and mix the ingredients well before serving. Garnish with chopped coriander leaves.

# Brinjal Chutney

**Ingredients**

| | |
|---|---|
| Brinjal | 1/4 kg |
| Cooking Oil | 1 tsp |
| Cumin Seeds | 1 tsp |
| Salt | to taste |
| Turmeric powder | 1/4 tsp |
| Green Chillies | 10-15 |
| Curry Leaves | to taste |
| Coriander Leaves | as required |
| Garlic | to taste |
| Tamarind | Lime sized |

**Process of preparation:** Cut the Brinjals into 4 pieces each, chop Green Chillies and fry them in pan and set aside. Take mixture of Garlic, Cumin and Tamarind, grind them finely and fry the paste in another pan. Now mix the already fried Brinjal and Chillies into this mixture of spices, blend them nicely and again grind all of them into a fine paste. Transfer to a bowl and garnish with chopped Coriander leaves. This Chutney does not need seasoning.

# Brinjal Tomato Curry

**Ingredients**

| | | | |
|---|---|---|---|
| Brinjal | 250 gms. | Curry leaves | As required |
| Tomatoes | 4 Nos. | Coriander leaves | As required |
| Cooking oil | 2 tbsps | Red Chilly powder | 1 tsp |
| Onions (sliced) | 2 Nos. | Salt | to taste |
| Cumin & Mustard seeds | as required | Turmeric powder | 1/4 tsp |

**Process of preparation**

Clean Brinjals and Tomatoes and cut into small pieces (brinjal – preferably in 2 or 4 pieces depending on size) and keep aside. Heat oil and add cumin & mustard seeds and curry leaves for seasoning. When seeds splutter, add onion to the oil and fry till onion turns brown. Now, put chopped Brinjal pieces to it and cook for a while till it is half cooked then add sliced tomatoes, followed by salt, Red Chilly powder, turmeric powder and stir it slowly that brinjal pieces remain intact. Garnish with chopped, Coriander, before removing from the stove. This curry is tasty along with both rice as well as Chapathis.

## Brinjal Sour Curry

**Ingredients**

| | |
|---|---|
| Brinjals | 1/4 kg |
| Green Chillies | 3 nos. (split) |
| Cooking Oil | 1 tsp |
| Cumin & Mustard seeds | as required |
| Curry Leaves | as required |
| Coriander Leaves | as required |
| Onion | 1 no. (sliced) |
| Salt | to taste |
| Red Chilli Powder | 1 tsp |
| Turmeric | 1/4 tsp |
| Tamarind | Lime sized |

**Process of preparation**

Cut Brinjals into 4 pieces, chop Onions, Green Chillies and set aside. Add Turmeric, Salt, Red Chilli powder, Tamarind pulp (prepared after soaking it in water for 1 hour before cooking) to the mixture of Brinjal, Onions and Green Chillies. Boil all the Ingredients together in a pressure cooker. Heat oil in a pan, add Cumin & Mustard seeds and Curry Leaves and tamper the curry with this seasoning. Now transfer the sour curry into a bowl and garnish with freshly chopped Coriander. This curry is suitable to be eaten along with rice.

## Brinjal Potato Curry

**Ingredients**

| | |
|---|---|
| Brinjal | 4 Nos. |
| Cumin & Mustard seeds | as required |
| Potatoes | 4 Nos. |
| Cooking oil | 2 tbsps |
| Red Chilly Powder | 1 tsp |
| Onion | 2 Nos. (sliced) |
| Salt | to taste |
| Green Chillies | 2 Nos. (split) |
| Turmeric | 1/4 tsp |
| Curry leaves | a few sprigs |

**Process of preparation**

Wash Brinjals and potatoes in water, peel and chop the potato and cut brinjals into 2 or 4 pieces depending on its size. Chop green Chillies, slice onions, and set aside in different bowls. Heat oil and add cumin and mustard seeds and curry leaves, When seasoning seeds splatter, add sliced onion, chopped green Chillies and saute till onion acquires brown color, Now, add potato pieces. When potatoes are half cooked, add brinjal pieces and salt, Chilly powder, and Turmeric powder and stir the contents slowly so that Brinjals and potatoes are not mashed in the curry. When cooking is done, garnish with chopped Coriander leaves and remove from the stove. This curry can be had with both rice as well as chapathis.

*Benefits*

- ✓ Takes care of your heart
- ✓ Improves cognitive function
- ✓ Helps to lose weight
- ✓ Helps treat anemia
- ✓ Helps to fight cancer
- ✓ Helps in digestion
- ✓ Good for your bones
- ✓ Useful during pregnancy
- ✓ Helps to manage diabetes

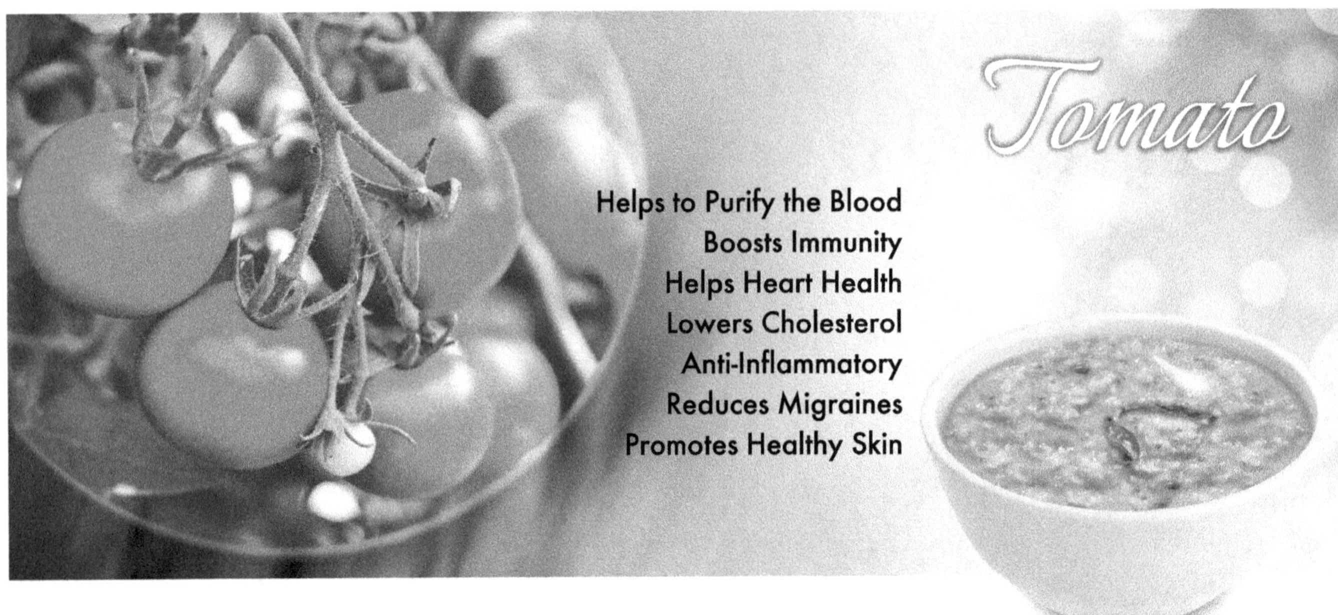



## Tomato Dal (Tomato with Lentils)

### Ingredients

| | | | |
|---|---|---|---|
| Red Gram | 1 cup | Cooking Oil | 2 tbsps |
| Cumin & Mustard seeds | as required | Curry leaves | as required |
| Coriander | as required | Onion | 1 no. |
| Green Chillies | 2 nos. | Ginger Pieces | ½ tsp |
| Red Chilli Powder | 1 tsp | Salt | to taste |
| Turmeric powder | 1/4 tsp | Tamarind | Lime sized |

### Process of preparation

Clean the tomatoes in water and chop them into small pieces and add Green Chillies, chopped Ginger, Red Chilli Powder, Turmeric and Tamarind pulp/juice (made from well soaked Tamarind in water). Boil all the ingredients in a pressure cooker along with red gram. After about 3 whistles, put off the stove, let the excess pressure recede, and slowly remove the lid of the pressure cooker. Add salt and mix it well. Heat oil in a pan and add Cumin & Mustard seeds and few Curry Leaves into it for seasoning purpose. Now add the Seasoned Oil in the cooked lentils, stir it nicely and garnish with chopped Coriander before serving.

## Tomato Spicy Curry

### Ingredients

| | | | |
|---|---|---|---|
| Tomato pieces | 2 cups | Coriander Leaves | as required |
| Cooking Oil | 2 tbsps | Turmeric Powder | 1/4 tsp |
| Cumin & Mustard seeds | as required | Red Chilli Powder | 1 tsp |
| Onion | 2 Nos. | Salt | to taste |
| Green Chillies | 2 Nos. | Curd | Little bit |
| Curry Leaves | as required | Garam Masala powder | 1 tsp |

### Process of preparation

Chop the tomatoes into small pieces and set aside. Heat some oil in a frying pan, add Cumin and Mustard seeds and Curry leaves into the hot Oil. To this add Onions, Green Chillies and wait till the Onions turn golden brown. To this add chopped Tomatoes followed by Salt, Turmeric, Garam Masala powder, Red Chilli Powder and stir the ingredients well. You can add curd if you wish to. This recipe goes well with Rice as well as Chapathis.

# Pumpkin

Cholesterol Free

Soidum Free

Good Source of Fibre

Fat Free

Calories

Carbs

Protein

Fiber

Fat

## Pumpkin Curry

### Ingredients

| | | | |
|---|---|---|---|
| Pumpkin pieces | 2 cups | Cooking Oil | 2 tbsps |
| Cumin & Mustard | as required | Onion | 1 no. (sliced) |
| Green Chillies | 3-4 nos. (chopped) | Curry Leaves | as required |
| Coriander Leaves | as required | Red Chilli Powder | 1 tsp |
| Salt | to taste | Turmeric Powder | 1/4 tsp |

### Process of preparation

Cut the Pumpkin and Onion into small pieces and set aside. Heat oil in a pan, and add Cumin & Mustard seeds and Curry Leaves for seasoning ,add chopped Onion  and Green Chillies as well as Ginger Garlic paste and a pinch of Garam Masala Powder to it. Next add Pumpkin pieces, Onion, Green Chillies to the seasoned oil, followed by Salt, Red Chilli Powder and Turmeric. Stir the contents and allow the ingredients to cook for a while and add a cup of milk. Cook it for some more time and garnish with chopped Coriander before removing from the stove. If desired, a little bit of jaggery can also be added to it. This recipe is very beneficial for children as it improves their eyesight. It is also a very tasty dish.

## Pumpkin Sour Curry

### Ingredients

| | | | |
|---|---|---|---|
| Pumpkin (Big Pieces) | 2 cups | Cooking Oil | 1 tbsp |
| Onion | 1 no. (sliced) | Green Chillies | 2 nos. (split) |
| Curry leaves | as required | Coriander Leaves | as required |
| Red Chilli Powder | 1 tsp | Salt | to taste |
| Turmeric Powder | 1/4 tsp | Tamarind | Lime sized |
| Cumin & Mustard seeds | as required | Jaggery | Little bit |

### Process of preparation

Cut Pumpkin into small pieces and set aside. Heat Oil in  a pan  and add cumin &mustard seeds along with Curry Leaves and allow the seeds to crackle. Add the chopped pumpkin pieces, followed by Salt, Red Chilly Powder, Turmeric powder and Tamarind, stir the contents and allow it to cook for some time. Add Jaggery to the ingredients and cook it further. Before removing from stove, garnish the Pumpkin Sour Curry with some freshly chopped Coriander Leaves.

This curry should not be consumed by those suffering from back pain and knee joint pains.

# Onion

## Onion Peas Curry

### Ingredients

| | | | |
|---|---|---|---|
| Raw Peas | 1 cup | Cooking Oil | 2 tbsps |
| Dried Mango Powder (Aamchur) | 1/2 tsp | Red Chilli Powder | 1 tsp |
| Cumin & Mustard Seeds | 1 tsp | Salt | to taste |
| Coriander Powder | 2 tsps | Turmeric | 1/4 tsp |
| Coriander Leaves | as required | Ginger pieces | 1 tsp |
| Onion | 1 no. (sliced) | tomatoes finely chopped | 2 nos |

### Process of preparation

Chop the Onion into small pieces and set aside. Heat oil in a non stick pan, add Cumin seeds & Mustard seeds and allow the seeds to crackle. Once they start spluttering , add chopped Onions and Green Chillis and stir till Onions turn brownish. Add chopped Ginger followed by peas, Red Chilli Powder and chopped tomato. Add Coriander Powder, Cumin Powder, Unripe Mango Powder (Aamchur) and Garam Masala Powder. Let it cook till tomatoes become totally soft and are easily crushed. If needed, you can sprinkle some water. Once all the ingredients are cooked well,  add Salt and cook for another 2-3 minutes. Garnish it with freshly chopped Coriander Leaves. This dish is not only very tasty but also very good for health.

## Onion Curry

### Ingredients

| | | | |
|---|---|---|---|
| Onion | 4 nos. (sliced) | Cooking Oil | 5 tbsps |
| Red Chilli Powder | ½ tsp | Salt | to taste |
| Bengal Gram flour | 3/4 cup | | |

### Process of preparation

Chop Onions into small pieces and set aside. Heat oil in a pan and add chopped Onion  and fry it till the pieces turn brown. Now add  Bengal Gram flour followed by Salt, Red Chilli Powder, Turmeric and stir well, remove the pan from the stove and serve. This dish is a good accompaniment with Phulkas. (Note while adding Bengal Gram flour, take care to see that the Onion and powder mixture is continuously stirred, so that the flour does not cuddle up or form lumps and is uniformly distributed along with the Onion pieces).

# *Cabbage*

Cabbage cools the body
and helps in the formation of Blood.
It also reduces heat in our brain and
gives us sound sleep.

## Cabbage Fry

**Ingredients**

| | | | |
|---|---|---|---|
| Cabbage (Finely Chopped) | 2 cups | Cooking Oil | 1 tbsp |
| Cumin & Mustard seeds | as required | Onion | 1 no. (sliced) |
| Green Chillies | 2 nos. (chopped) | Curry Leaves | as required |
| Coriander Leaves | as required | Red Chilli Powder | 1 tsp |
| Salt | to taste | Turmeric Powder | ¼ tsp |
| Cloves | 2 nos. | Ginger | small piece |

**Process of preparation**

Chop the Cabbage into small fine slices and set aside. Heat oil in a pan and add Cumin & Mustard seeds, Curry leaves and Cloves in it for seasoning. When the seeds splutter add Onions & Green Chilli, wait till the Onions turn brown. Now add Chopped Cabbage followed by salt, Turmeric powder and stir. Once the cabbage is nicely cooked, add crushed Garlic and Chilli powder and mix well. Before removing from the flame, garnish with freshly chopped Coriander leaves.

## Cabbage Chutney

**Ingredients**

| | | | |
|---|---|---|---|
| Cabbage (finely Grated) | 2 cups | Green Chillies | 10-12 Nos. |
| Curry leaves | a few sprigs | Coriander leaves | as required |
| Garlic | 4 pods | Cooking oil | 1 tbsp |
| Salt | To taste | Cumin Powder | 1 tsp |
| Tamarind | Lime sized | | |

**Process of preparation**

Chop cabbage finely. Chop Green Chillies to pieces and set aside. Heat oil and add chopped cabbage and Green Chillies to it and allow it to cook for a few minutes. Remove from the stove after it is cooked take a few Green Chillies, soaked Tamarind (soaked one hour before cooking) Salt, Garlic, Curry leaves, and Cumin powder and grind all these together. Add this mixture to the pre-cooked Cabbage and Green Chillies, and grind again but coarsely. Add Coriander leaves (chopped) for garnishing and transfer into a serving bowl.

This chutney does not need seasoning with oil and seeds. This chutney can be had with rice, Chapathi as well as snacks.

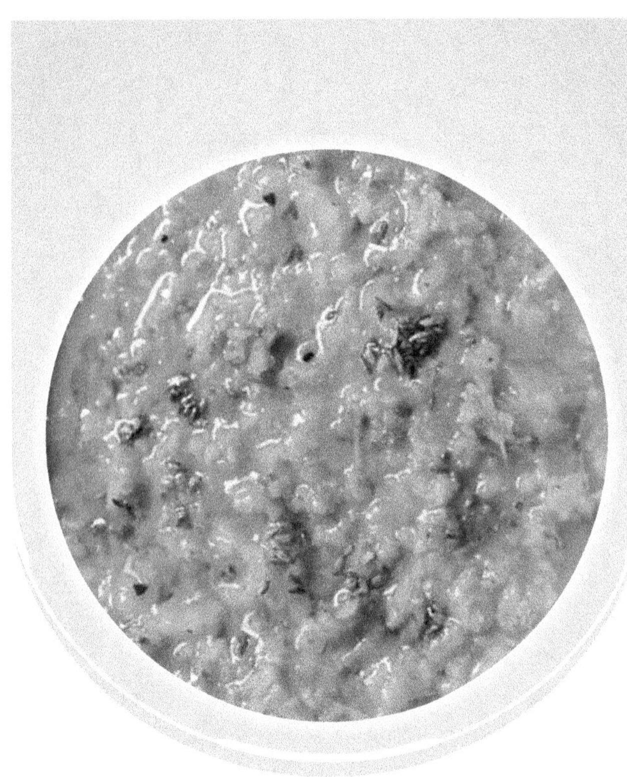

## Cabbage
## Split Bengal Gram Curry

**Ingredients**

| | |
|---|---|
| Chopped Cabbage | 2 cups |
| Split Bengal Gram | 1.5 cups |
| Cooking Oil | 2 tsps |
| Red Chilli Powder | 1 tsp |
| Cumin & Mustard seeds | 1 tsp |
| Salt | to taste |
| Onion | 2 nos. (sliced) |
| Turmeric Powder | ¼ tsp |
| Green Chillies | 4 nos. (chopped) |

**Process of preparation**

Chop the Onion and Cabbage into small pieces and boil and set aside. Soak Split Bengal Gram in a bowl and set aside. Heat oil in a pan, add Cloves, Cumin & Mustard seeds and Curry Leaves for seasoning. Next add previously soaked Split Bengal Gram followed by Red Chilli Powder, Turmeric and water and stir well. After the Bengal Gram is half cooked, add the boiled Cabbage. When the Bengal Gram and cabbage are totally cooked, add Salt to taste and serve. Garnish with coriander leaves.

## Cabbage Spiced Curry

**Ingredients**

| | |
|---|---|
| Cabbage | 1 cup |
| Red Chilli Powder | 1 tsp |
| Onion | 1 No. (sliced) |
| Salt | To taste |
| Green Chillies | 4 Nos. (chopped) |
| Turmeric | 1/4 tsp |
| Curry leaves | A few sprigs |
| Cloves | 2 Nos. |
| Coriander leaves | as required |
| Garam Masala | 1 tspoon |
| Mint leaves | as required |
| Cardamom | 1 No. |
| Cumin & Mustard seeds | as Required |
| Cinnamon | 1 inch long |
| Cooking Oil | 1 tbsp |
| Ginger Garlic paste | 2 tsps |

**Process of preparation**

Wash Cabbage and other vegetables, chop the Cabbage, Onion, Green Chillies, Mint and Coriander leaves into small pieces, and set aside.

Heat oil in pan, add mustard, cumin, cinnamon and cardamom, when the seeds splutter, add sliced onion and green chilly to it. When onions turn brown in color, add Ginger Garlic paste and after a while, when the raw smell of the paste subsides, add chopped cabbage followed by salt, Red Chilli powder and Turmeric and stir all the ingredients thoroughly, wait till the Cabbage is cooked and softened and add Garam Masala powder to it. Cook it for a few more minutes and sprinkle chopped coriander and mint leaves over the curry before removing from the stove.

This curry is a good combination with both rice as well as Chapathis.

## Cauliflower Curry

### Ingredients

| | | | |
|---|---|---|---|
| Cauliflower (small pieces) | 2 cups | Tomato Pieces | 1 cup |
| Onion | 2 Nos. (sliced) | Green Chillies | 2 Nos. (split) |
| Cooking oil | 1 tsp | Cumin & Mustard | As required |
| Coriander leaves | a few twigs | Mint leaves | a few twigs |
| Red Chilli Powder | 1 tsp | Turmeric Powder | 1/4 tsp |
| Salt | ½ tsp | Cinnamon powder | 1 tsp |
| Curry leaves | a few | | |

### Process of preparation

Cut cauliflower pieces and soak the flowers in hot water along with salt and turmeric powder to remove any hidden pests or impurities. Slice onions. Heat oil in a pan  add cumin and mustard seeds and curry leaves.  When the seeds crackle add chopped onions and Green Chillies to the seasoned oil. When onions turns brown in color, add sliced tomatoes to it, and after a minute add cauliflower pieces (remove from water and squeezed lightly), Red Chilli Powder, Salt and Turmeric powder and finally cinnamon powder and stir the ingredients before removing from the stove, add chop coriander and mint leaves for garnish.

# Meal Maker

- ✓ Improves bone health
- ✓ Prevents Cancer
- ✓ Boosts heart health
- ✓ Improves blood circulation
- ✓ Improves metabolic activity
- ✓ Controls diabetes
- ✓ Boosts digestive health
- ✓ Helps in preventing birth defects

## Meal Maker Curry

**Ingredients**

| | | | |
|---|---|---|---|
| Meal Maker | 200 gm | Tomatoes (Big sized) | 2 Nos. |
| Onion | 3 Nos. (sliced) | Cooking oil | 2 tbsps |
| Green Chillies | 3 Nos. (chopped) | Cumin and Mustard seeds | As required |
| Salt | as required | Garlic | 10 pods |
| Garam Masala | ½ tsp | Red Chilli Powder | ½ tsp |
| Ginger | 20 gms | Tomato ketchup | 1 tsp |
| Chaat Masala | Little bit | Dried Mango powder | 1/2 tsp |

**Process of preparation**

Soak meal maker in water for 3 hours. Remove from water and squeeze out the excess water. Grind ginger, garlic and Green Chillies to a paste. Heat oil in a pan and add ground paste.

 followed by chopped onion and fry the onion till it becomes brownish. Then add tomato pulp and allow it to cook for some time. Add chaat masala, garam masala powder, Chilly powder, Dried Mango (Aamchur) powder, Tomato ketchup and Meal Maker balls, stir all the ingredients thoroughly. Then add salt and water  and allow it to simmer till meal maker becomes soft. Before removing from stove, garnish with chopped coriander leaves. This curry can be relished with rice or  chapathis.

✓ Strengthens Immune System

✓ Protects against Cancer

✓ Aids in Healthy Digestion

✓ Maintains Healthy Eye & Skin

✓ Boosts Energy

✓ Lower High Blood Pressure

✓ Controls Asthma

✓ Strengthens the Bone

✓ Prevents Anemia

✓ Maintains Healthy Thyroid

# Jack Fruit

## Jackfruit Curry

### Ingredients

| | | | |
|---|---|---|---|
| Jack Fruit pieces | 1/4 Kg. | Poppy seeds | 1 tsp |
| Cloves | ½ tsp | Cooking oil | 3 tbsps |
| Cardamom | 2 Nos. | Onion | 2 Nos. (sliced) |
| Red Chilly Powder | 1 tsp | Cumin seeds | ½ tsp |
| Salt | To taste | Coriander seeds | 1 tsp |
| Cumin & Mustard seeds | 2 inch long | Ginger Garlic paste | 1 tsp |
| Turmeric | 1/4 tsp | Green Chillies | 4 Nos. (chopped) |

### Process of preparation

Cut Jackfruit into cubes and chop Green Chillis and onion and set aside. Heat oil in a pan, add the Jackfruit cubes to the hot oil and fry till color of cubes changes. Remove from oil and keep it in a bowl. Add chopped onion, and Green Chillies, followed by ginger garlic paste to the seasoned oil. Then add fried jackfruit cubes, Salt and Red Chilli powder and simmer with the pan covered by a lid. Take Cloves, Cardamom, Cinnamon, Coriander seeds, poppy seeds and cumin seeds and grind in a mixer and set aside in a small bowl. Add this ground paste to the pre-cooked jackfruit cubes, and also ½ glass of water, and again cook the ingredients, when the jackfruit cubes are completely cooked and become soft then put off the stove and garnish the curry with chopped coriander. This curry will be tasty with both rice and chapathis.

Mixed Vegetable Curries

Capsicum has a unique quality of reducing cholesterol from our body. This apart, any dish made from this vegetable is very tasty.

## Capsicum - Raw (Green) Peas Curry

### Ingredients

| | | | |
|---|---|---|---|
| Capsicum pieces | 1 cup | Curry leaves | As required |
| Split Bengal Gram | 1 cup | Mustard seeds | 1 Tsp |
| White sesame seeds | 2 Tsp | Asafoetida | little bit |
| Raw (green) Peas | 1 cup | Coriander leaves | as required |
| Jaggery | a little bit | Cumin Seeds | ½ Tsp |
| Dried Red Chillies | 4 Nos. | Coconut grated | 2 Tsp |
| Coriander seeds | 2 Tsp | Turmeric powder | Little bit |
| Cooking Oil | 1 Tsp | Tamarind Juice | 5 gms. |

### Process of preparation

Take 3/4th cup of water in a cooker and boil raw  peas in it for 5 minutes. Heat oil in a frying pan and roast Coriander seeds, sesame seeds, red (dried) Chillies, split  bengal gram and Asafoetida. Fry all ingredients together till they emanate pleasant smell. Add grated coconut and tamarind and grind the roasted ingredients to a paste with little water. Heat oil in a pan, add mustard ,cumin seeds and curry leaves for seasoning. Add the chopped capsicum pieces and some water and boil it for 10 minutes and then remove boiled capsicum pieces and set aside. Add salt, jaggery and ground paste to  the pan, add 1/2 cup of water and allow the ingredients to  come to a boil. Reduce the flame and add raw peas and capsicum, stir it nicely and cook for 5 minutes till the gravy becomes thick. This recipe can be relished with rice, chapathis as well as pooris.

# Cabbage - Tomato Curry

**Ingredients**

| | | | |
|---|---|---|---|
| Cabbage (finely chopped) | 2 cups | Chopped tomato | 1 no |
| Salt | to taste | Coriander leaves | As required |
| Green Chillies | 2 Nos. (chopped) | Cooking oil | 2 tsp |
| Cumin & Mustard seeds | for seasoning | Chilly powder | 1tsp |
| Curry leaves | as required | Chopped Onion | 1 No. |

**Process of preparation**

Heat oil in a pan, add cumin and mustard seeds, curry leaves, allow the seeds to splutter and then add chopped onion and green Chillies and stir, after a minute add cabbage and tomato pieces to the seasoned oil. Add salt and Chilly powder to the ingredients and stir thoroughly and let the ingredients simmer for a few minutes. When the vegetables cook properly and become soft, then garnish the curry with chopped coriander leaves and serve hot. This curry will be tastier if we add raw peas.

# Lady's Finger Capsicum Curry

**Ingredients**

| | |
|---|---|
| Capsicum | 2 nos. |
| Salt | To taste |
| Lady's Finger (Okra) | 1/4 kg. |
| Ajinomoto | little bit |
| Green Chillies | 5 nos. (chopped) |
| Soya Sauce | 1 tsp |
| Cooking Oil | 3 tsp |
| Cornflower | 1 tsp |
| Garlic Ginger | 1 tsp each |
| Sugar | Little bit |
| Onion | 2 Nos. (sliced) |

**Process of preparation:** Wash, dry and chop Okra. Wash Capsicum, remove its seeds and cut into pieces. In a small container mix half of soya sauce and half of Corn Flour, and also salt and keep aside. Heat oil in a pan and add ginger and garlic to it and sauté for a minute, then add Green Chilly, Onion and capsicum pieces to it and sauté for one more minute, add soya sauce to it and again sauté the mixture. Add Okra pieces, allow the pieces to cook for a minute and then add the mixture of corn flour and water, salt sugar and ajinomoto and cook all ingredients for some more time till the gravy become thick. Finally, before removing from the stove, sprinkle chopped coriander over the curry and serve. This curry goes well with fried rice.

# Capsicum - Tomato Curry

**Ingredients**

| | |
|---|---|
| Capsicum | 1 cup |
| Red Chilly powder | 1 tsp |
| Tomatoes | 1 cup |
| Turmeric | 1/4 tsp |
| Onion | 2 nos. (sliced) |
| Salt | To taste |
| Green Chillies Chopped | 2 nos. |
| Cooking oil | 1 tsp |
| Coriander leaves | A few twigs |
| Cumin Mustard | As required |
| Curry leaves | A few sprigs |
| Curd | ½ cup |

**Process of preparation**

Wash and chop Capsicum and cut Tomatoes into small pieces and slice onions. Chop Green Chillies, coriander leaves and set aside in different bowls. Heat oil in a pan and add cumin & Mustard seeds and curry leaves and when seeds splutter, add sliced onion, green chilly and when onion becomes brownish, add chopped tomato, capsicum, salt, chilly powder, and turmeric powder. In the end when the curry is almost done, add curd to it, then garnish with chopped coriander and remove from stove. This curry is very tasty along with both rice as well as chapathis.

# Capsicum Split Bengal Gram Curry

**Ingredients**

| | | | |
|---|---|---|---|
| Capsicum pieces | 2 cups | Ginger Garlic Paste | 2 tsps |
| Chilly powder | 1 tsp | Cumin & Mustard seeds | a few |
| Soaked  Bengal gram | 1/4 cup | Garam Masala powder | 1tsp |
| Turmeric | 1/4 tsp | Coconut | Little bit |
| Onion | 2 nos. (sliced) | Coriander leaves | a few |
| Cooking oil | 2 tsp | Curd | ½ cup |
| Green Chillies | 4 (chopped) | Mint leaves | a few |
| Salt | to taste | | |

**Process of preparation**

Wash and chop capsicum, green Chillies and coriander leaves .Grind coconut along with green chilies, coriander leaves and soaked Bengal gram and curd. Heat oil in a pan add the cumin and mustard seeds . Once the seeds crackle, add chopped onion, followed by mint leaves and ginger garlic paste and fry all items. Then add capsicum pieces. When these pieces are half cooked add the ground mixture followed by salt, red Chilly powder, and turmeric and allow it to simmer well. After it is done, garnish the curry with chopped Coriander. This curry will be better if it is in semi liquid stage than concentrated. This dish goes with rice as well as Chapathis.

# Capsicum Potato Curry

**Ingredients**

| | | | |
|---|---|---|---|
| Capsicum (pieces) | 2 cups | Mint leaves (chop) | ½ a cup |
| Potato (pieces) | 1 cup | Chilly powder | 1 span |
| Onion (chopped) | 2 nos. | Turmeric powder | 1/4 tsp |
| Green Chillis (Pieces) | 4 | Cooking oil | 2 tbsps |
| Coriander | A few twigs | Salt | to taste |
| Curry leaves | A few sprigs | Cumin & Mustard seeds | As required |

**Process of preparation**

Wash capsicum and potato (peel of its skin) and cut into pieces. Place a frying pan over a lighted stove, pour oil in it and when oil is heated, put cumin and Mustard and curry leaves in it for seasoning. When seeds splatter, add potato pieces (with skin peeled off), Onion, green Chillis, followed by salt, Chilly powder, turmeric powder, and let all ingredients be stirred and simmer, when half cooked, add capsicum pieces & chopped mint leaves and cook it for a few minutes - Garnish with coriander and serve with either rice or chapathis.

# Raw Peas Tomato Curry

**Ingredients**

| | | | |
|---|---|---|---|
| Raw Peas | 1 cup | Coriander leaves | As required |
| Cumin powder | 1/4 tsp | Sesame seeds | as required |
| Tomatoes | 250 gm | Coconut | As required |
| Cumin & Mustard seeds | As required | Green Chillies | 4 nos. (chopped) |
| Cooking oil | 2 tsps | Turmeric powder | 1/4 tsp |
| Curry leaves | As required | Salt | to taste |
| | | Onion | 2 Nos. (sliced) |

**Process of preparation**

Wash peas and tomatoes. Slice tomatoes, onion and green Chillies. Heat oil in a pan, add cumin and mustard seeds and curry leaves, once the seeds crackle, add sliced onion and green Chillies and fry the ingredients till onion turns brownish. Add tomatoes pieces and raw peas, sesame seeds, coconut, followed by salt, Chilly powder and cumin powder, turmeric powder and stir the contents. Simmer for a few minutes till the peas are cooked and softened. Garnish with chopped coriander leaves and remove from stove. This dish can be enjoyed with both rice and Chapathis as well.

# Broad Beans - Tomato Curry

**Ingredients**

| | | | |
|---|---|---|---|
| Broad Beans | 250 gms | Salt | To taste |
| Red Chilly Powder | 1 tsp | Green Chillis | As required |
| Tomatoes (Cut in pieces) | 4 nos. | Cumin & Mustard seeds | As required |
| Turmeric powder | 1/4 tsp | Coriander leaves | As required |
| Onion (sliced) | 2 nos. | | |

**Process of preparation**

String and Cut the Broad Beans into small pieces. Boil in a pressure cooker along with some salt and set aside. Heat oil, add cumin and mustard seeds along with few curry leaves. When the seeds crackle, add sliced onion and green Chillies to it. Wait till the onion turns brown. Then add tomato pieces, followed by salt, turmeric powder and Red Chilly powder. Now after tomatoes are half cooked, add boiled broad Beans and simmer for 5mins. Finally, before removing from stove, garnish with chopped coriander leaves and serve the tasty curry.

## 2nd Variant (Method) Preparation of Curry

Raw Peas should be boiled and this can be cooked in combination with various vegetables likes Cabbage, Cauliflower, Brinjal, Potatoes etc., In this case there is no need to add groundnuts, or coconut or sesame seeds. We need not add water to this curry, since the tomato adds water to the curry in the form of its juice. Cook this curry on slow flame and enjoy its flavor.

# Drumstick - Yellow Cucumber (Dosakaya Curry)

**Ingredients**

| | | | |
|---|---|---|---|
| Drumsticks | 3 nos. | Turmeric powder | 1/4 tsp |
| Red Chilly powder | 1 tsp | Cooking oil | 2 tsp |
| Yellow cucumber | 1 no. | Cumin & Mustard seeds | as required |
| Salt | To taste | Coriander leaves | As required |
| Onions | 2 Nos. (sliced) | Green Chillies | 3 Nos. (chopped) |

**Process of preparation**

Wash and cut drumsticks. Peel the skin and cut yellow cucumber into pieces. Slice onions, green Chillies and set aside in separate bowls Heat oil in a pan and add cumin and mustard seeds and when the seeds splutter, add drumsticks pieces, green chilly pieces, onion pieces and cucumber pieces and let all ingredients simmer for a few minutes Add salt, Chilly powder and turmeric powder and cook till the vegetables are cooked soft. Garnish it with chopped coriander leaves and remove from the stove. This curry can be had with rice.

# Mushrooms - Kenaf (Gongura) Leaves

**Ingredients**

| | | | |
|---|---|---|---|
| Kenaf (Gongura) leaves | 3 cups | Mushrooms | 200 gms |
| Red Chilli powder | ½ tsp | Turmeric powder | 1/4 tsp |
| Cooking oil | 50 gms | Green Chillis | 6 nos. |
| Salt | To taste | Ginger-Garlic paste | 2 tsps |
| Onion (sliced) | 3 nos. | Coriander leaves | A few twigs |

**Process of preparation**

Wash the mushrooms thoroughly and chop into pieces and set aside. Wash Kenaf leaves and boil the leaves in water along with green Chillies. Heat oil add ginger-garlic paste, followed by salt, red Chilly powder and Turmeric powder. Stir and add the chopped mushroom pieces, boiled Kenaf leaves and simmer for a while. When the curry is done garnish with chopped coriander leaves.

# Avial (Kerala Dish)

**Ingredients**

| | | | |
|---|---|---|---|
| Ash Gourd | 100 grm. | Red Pumpkin | 100 grm. |
| Yarn | 100 grm. | Medium Potato | 1 no. |
| French Beans | 10 to 12 nos. | Medium Carrots | 3 nos. |
| Drumsticks | 1 no. | Raw Banana Medium | ½ |
| Medium Onion | 2 nos. (sliced) | Curry Leaves | 10 nos. |
| Turmeric Powder | ¼ spoon | Sore curd whipped | 1½ cup |
| Salt to | taste | Spice Paste | |
| Coconut grated | 1½ cup | Green Chillies | 4 nos. |
| Cumin Seeds | 3 tsp. | Ginger+Garlic Paste | 1 tsp. |

**Process of preparation**

Grind ingredients for the spice paste and keep aside. Wash, Peel and cut all the vegetables to one inch pieces. Add a pinch of turmeric powder and place them into a vessel. Cook the vegetables for 15-20 minutes till the vegetables are tender. Add the spice paste, salt and stir for a few minutes. After drying the excess moisture add the whipped curd and curry leaves. Remove from the heat serve it with rice.

To prevent curdling do not boil the avial after adding the curd. Avial is seasoned with a table spoon of coconut oil before taking it off the heat.

Bulbous
Roots

# *Carrots*

We all know that Carrot has Vitamin "A" in abundance. The pulp of carrot is used in preparation of curries, chutneys, salads, as well as mixed with Chapathy dough andidly dough for preparing Chapathis and Idlys.

- ✓ Improves eye sight
- ✓ Prevents heart diseases
- ✓ Reduces high blood pressure
- ✓ Maintains good digestive health
- ✓ Regulates blood sugar levels
- ✓ Prevents macular degeneration
- ✓ Reduces risk of cancer & stroke
- ✓ Boosts immune system

## Carrot Spicy Curry (Khorma)

### Ingredients

| | | | |
|---|---|---|---|
| Carrot pieces | 1 cup | Corn kernels | 1 cup |
| Cooking oil | 2 tbsps | Turmeric | 1/4 tsp |
| Potato pieces | 1 cup | Tomatoes (pieces) | 1 cup |
| Ginger Garlic paste | 2 tsps | Cardamom | 2 nos |
| Raw Peas | 1 cup | Cloves | 2 nos. |
| Curd | 1 cup | Salt | to taste |
| Capsicum (pieces) | ½ a cup | Cinnamon | Little bit |
| Red Chilly powder | 1 tsp | Garam Masala powder | 1 tsp |

### Process of preparation

Cut Potato, Capsicum, tomatoes and carrots. Boil potatoes, and tomatoes in salted water. Boil the Corn kernels and set aside. Heat oil in a frying pan add cumin and mustard seeds. Once the seeds crackle add cinnamon, cloves, cardamom, ginger garlic paste and saute for 1minute. Add all boiled vegetables, carrot, capsicum, corn kernels, peas, followed by salt, turmeric red chilly powder, garam masala powder and finally whipped curd and stir well. Cook all ingredients on a slow flame till the vegetables, corn and peas are properly cooked and softened. Garnish with chopped coriander before serving. Please make sure that the curry or khorma is in semi solid state and not fully concentrated.

This khorma (spicy curry) is everybody's favorite and is compatible with both rice as well as chapathis.

## Grated Carrot Curry

**Ingredients**

| | | | |
|---|---|---|---|
| Grated carrot | 2 cups | Red Chilly powder | 1 tsp |
| Dried / fresh coconut | ½ cup | Green Chilly | 4 nos. (chopped) |
| Cooking oil | 2 tbsps | Curry leaves | A few sprigs |
| Cumin Mustard Seeds | As required | Coriander leaves | A few twigs |
| Onions (chopped into pieces) | 2 nos. | Salt | to taste |
| Turmeric powder | 1/4 tsp | Garlic | 2 nos. |

**Process of preparation**

Wash carrots and grate it and set aside. Grate coconut and transfer to a small bowl. Chop onions and green Chillies and set aside in a bowl. Heat oil in a frying pan, add cumin and mustard seeds. Once seeds crackle add chopped onions and green Chillies and stir till onion turns to brownish color. Add grated carrot, followed by salt and turmeric powder and allow these to cook for a while. Next add crushed garlic (after peeling off its skin), chilly powder and coconut and stir the ingredients to blend well and let contents simmer for a minute. Garnish with chopped coriander, before removing from stove and serve hot.

# Kanda

## (Elephant Yam, Suran)

With Kanda, a bulbous root, we can cook varieties of Curries and chutneys

## Kanda Curry

**Ingredients**

| | | | |
|---|---|---|---|
| Kanda | 250 gms | Onion | 1 No. (sliced) |
| Garlic | 5 pods | Salt | to taste |
| Cooking oil | 3 tbsps | Green Chillies | 2 Nos. (chopped) |
| Red Chilly powder | 1 tsp | Curry leaves | A few sprigs |
| Cumin & Mustard seeds | As required | Coriander | A few twigs |
| Turmeric | 1/4 tsp | | |

**Process of preparation**

Wash and cut Kanda into 4 big pieces and boil in a pressure cooker (with proportionate water) till you hear 2 whistles of cooker and set aside. Cut Onions and Green Chillies into small pieces. Open the pressure cooker lid and take out boiled Kanda pieces and remove the skin. Then cut into smaller pieces again. Heat oil in a frying pan ,add Cumin and Mustard Seeds as well as Curry Leaves for seasoning. When the seeds start crackling, add chopped Onion and Green Chillies to the oil and fry Onion till it changes its color to brown. Next step is to add boiled Kanda pieces without skin, followed by Salt and Turmeric. Sauté the ingredients. After 5 minutes of cooking add crushed skinless Garlic pods and Red Chilly Powder, Simmer for 10 minutes, garnish with chopped Coriander leaves and remove the pan from the stove.

# Kanda (Elephant Foot Yam) Sour Curry

**Ingredients**

| | | | |
|---|---|---|---|
| Kanda | 250 gms | Red Chilly powder | 1 tsp |
| Onion | 1 no. | Turmeric Powder | 1/4 tsp |
| Cumin & Mustard Seeds | As required | Salt | to taste |
| Cooking oil | 4 nos. | Tamarind | Lime sized |
| Curry leaves | A few sprigs | Jaggery | ½ cup |
| Coriander leaves | A few twigs | | |

**Process of preparation**

Wash and cut Kanda into 4 big pieces and boil in a pressure cooker with sufficient water till 2 whistles of cooker. Slice the Onion and Green Chillies into small pieces. Remove Kanda from cooker, peel off its skin, cut in small pieces. In a pan add Salt, Chilly powder, Turmeric and extracted pulp/juice of Tamarind, along with Onion, Kanda and Green Chillies and sufficient water and boil all the ingredients together. After it is boiled, add powdered Jaggery to the curry. Season the curry by adding mustard cumin and curry leaves to hot oil. When the seeds crackle, pour the Kanda curry in the seasoned oil. This curry goes well with rice.

✓ Controls Blood Sugar
✓ Anti-Cancer properties
✓ Boosts immune system
✓ Improves Blood Circulation
✓ Reduces Fatigue
✓ Improves Digestive Health
✓ Healthy Heart
✓ Improves Vision
✓ Excellent Skin health
✓ Weight Loss

# Colocasia Fry

**Ingredients**

| | | | |
|---|---|---|---|
| Colocasia | 250 gms | Green Chillies | 2 nos. |
| Curry leaves | A few sprigs | Red Chilly Powder | 1 tsp |
| Cooking oil | 1 tbsp | Garlic | 5 pods |
| Coriander leaves | A few twigs | Turmeric | 1/4 tsp |
| Onion | 1 no. (sliced) | Cumin & Mustard seeds | As required |
| Salt | To taste | | |

**Process of preparation**

Wash Colocasia to remove mud etc. and boil in a pressure cooker till 2 whistles. Peel skin of the boiled Colocasia and cut into round / Circular shaped thin slices. Slice onions and cut Green Chillies in small pieces and keep them in a bowl separately. Heat oil and add cumin and mustard seeds and curry leaves. When the seeds crackle add sliced Onion and Green Chillies, wait till onion turns to brown color and then add the Colocasia pieces, followed by Salt, Red Chilly powder and Turmeric powder, along with Crushed Garlic pieces. Mix everything well and  allow it to cook till Colocasia pieces become soft. Garnish with chopped coriander and serve. This tasty dish can be had along with rice.

# Colocasia Sour Curry

**Ingredients**

| | | | |
|---|---|---|---|
| Colocasia | 250 gm | Red Chilly powder | ½ tsp |
| Cooking oil | As required | Turmeric powder | 1/4 tsp |
| Cumin & Mustard seeds | As required | Salt | to taste |
| Onion | 1 no. (sliced) | Tamarind | Lime sized |
| Green Chillies | 3 nos. (chopped) | Jaggery | A little bit |
| Coriander leaves | A few twigs | | |

**Process of preparation**

Boil Colocasia (after washing it thoroughly) in a pressure cooker till they become soft. Peel of the skin of boiled Colocasia and cut into round circular pieces. Soak Tamarind in a bowl half an hour in advance before cooking, remove it and squeeze it to obtain its juice. Take oil in a frying pan, heat it and add Cumin & Mustard seeds along with Curry leaves and wait till the seeds crackle. Add Onion and Green Chillies to the Seasoned Oil and wait till Onions turn brownish. Add  Colocasia, followed by Salt, Red Chilly Powder, Turmeric powder as well as Tamarind juice, one after the other and stir the ingredients. When Colocasia pieces are fully cooked and become soft, add 1/4th cup of jaggery to it, mix  and continue to cook for a while till the gravy becomes dense/thick. It is advisable that this curry is seasoned in the end with oil and seeds only after it is fully cooked.

# Radish

Radish is a nutritious vegetable and very good for our health. Radish also prevents growth of worms in our stomach but most people are not aware of this vegetable and its benefits. However, of late, people are gaining knowledge about its benefits and are using it. In Rajasthan and Uttar Pradesh people eat this vegetable in raw form. One of the popular preparations using radish is Chapathis with grated Radish.

Radish is also used for cooking Dal, sambars, and curries, as well as chutneys.

# Radish Curry

**Ingredients**

| | | | |
|---|---|---|---|
| Radish finely chopped | 1 cup | Green Chillies | 2 nos. (chopped) |
| Red Gram Dal | 1 cup | Curry leaves | A few sprigs |
| Cooking Oil | 1 tsp | Coriander leaves | few twigs |
| Cumin & Mustard seeds | As required | Red Chillis Powder | 1 tsp |
| Onion (sliced) | 1 no. | Turmeric powder | 1/4 tsp |
| Salt | to taste | | |

**Process of preparation**

Place all the cut vegetables including green chillies  in a pressure cooker along with dhal, Red Chilly Powder and Turmeric, add sufficient water to enable boiling of these vegetables until 3 whistles of cooker. Pour some oil in a frying pan, allow it to heat up and add cumin, mustard seeds and curry leaves. Once the seeds crackle, add sliced Onion, Green Chillies. When Onion turns brown, add boiled radish, dhal and spices, salt and cook for a few more minutes. Garnish before removing from stove.

# Radish Chutney

**Ingredients**

| | | | |
|---|---|---|---|
| Radish grated | 250 gm | Garlic | 4 pods |
| Cooking oil | 2 tsbps | Salt | To taste |
| Cumin & Mustard seeds | 2 tsps | Turmeric powder | 1 tsp |
| Green Chillies | 10 nos. | Tamarind | Lime sized |
| Curry leaves | A few sprigs | Coriander leaves | A few twigs |

**Process of preparation**

Grate radish or chop into fine pieces and chop Chillies and set aside. Now cook Radish and Green Chillies in a pan adding a little water. After radish is cooked, let it cool and then add tamarind, Salt, Garlic (crushed) & Cumin Powder and grind all these together. Heat oil in a stove, add Cumin and Mustard seeds and Curry leaves for seasoning. Add the chopped Onion and Chilly and wait till onion turns brownish. Now add the cooked Radish & Spices mixture to the seasoned oil and garnish with chopped Coriander.

## 2nd Variant

Take Red Chilly seeds, Cumin seeds, 2 tspoonsful of Sesame seeds and roast all these together and grind to a paste. Add this ground mixture to the cooked Radish mixture and grind all of these together in a grinder and finally garnish with chopped Coriander leaves. There is no need to season the chutney.

# Potato Curry

**Ingredients**

| | | | |
|---|---|---|---|
| Potato | 250 gm | Curry leaves | a few sprigs |
| Cooking oil | 100 ml | Coriander leaves | a few twigs |
| Cumin & Mustard seeds | As required | Onion | 2 nos. (sliced) |
| Garlic | 4 pods | Green Chillies | 4 nos. (chopped) |
| Salt | To taste | Turmeric powder | 1/4 tsp |

**Process of preparation**

Boil Potatoes in a pressure cooker with sufficient water till two whistles, then remove potatoes, let these cool and then peel the skin and chop potatoes. Slice Onion and chop Green Chillies. Heat oil in a pan, add cumin and mustard seeds and curry leaves in it for seasoning. Next add sliced Onion, Green Chillies and boiled Potatoes, followed by Salt and Turmeric powder and mix well. After the ingredients simmer for a few minutes, add peeled and crushed Garlic. Simmer for a few minutes and then garnish it with chopped coriander leaves.

## Potato Khorma

### Ingredients

| | | | |
|---|---|---|---|
| Potato | 250 gm | Onion | 3 nos. |
| Poppy Seeds | 1 tsp | Salt | to taste |
| Cooking oil | 2 tbsps | Green Chillies | 4 nos. |
| Curd | 1 cup | Cashew nuts | 10 nos. |
| Cumin & Mustard seeds | as required | Cloves | 2 nos. |
| Ginger Garlic paste | 1 tsp | Cardamom | 2 nos. |
| Garam Masala | 1 tsp | | |

### Process of preparation

Boil Potatoes in a pressure cooker for 2 whistles. After letting it cool, peel and chop potatoes into big pieces and set aside. Slice onions. Grind poppy seeds, cloves, cardamom, cinnamon and cashew nuts to paste. Heat oil in a frying pan and add Cloves, Crushed Cardamom, Cinnamon. Next add sliced Onion and Green Chilly ,Ginger-Garlic paste and poppy seeds paste and sauté further. Then add Salt, Turmeric Powder, and Curd, and chopped Potato pieces and stir all the ingredients thoroughly so as to blend them properly. Let the curry simmer till gravy is formed. If the gravy is too thick then add water to dilute it. Finally, garnish with chopped coriander. This curry is very tasty with rice, Chapathis and Pooris.

## Potato Benefits

| | |
|---|---|
| Rich in Vit C, B6, Copper & Manganese | Liver cleansing |
| Helps control Blood Sugar levels | Low in Sodium |
| Best energy producing veggie | High in Fibre & Vitamin A |
| Resists stroke & heart attack | Prevent kidney stones |
| Reduces inflammation | Improves Brain health |

Leafy
Vegetables

# Leafy Vegetables Special

**Ingredients**

| | | | |
|---|---|---|---|
| Amaranthus (Thotakura) | 2 bunches | Turmeric Powder | 1 tsp |
| Ginger pieces | 1tsp | Brinjals | 2 nos. |
| Basalae (Pulla Bachhali leaves) | 1 Bunch | Salt | To taste |
| Red Chilly Powder | 1 tsp | Potato | 1 no. |
| Tomatoes | 2 nos. | Split Bengal Gram | 1 cup |

**Process of preparation**

Wash leafy Vegetables well and chop the leaves. Cut all vegetables in small pieces and set aside in different bowls. Soak Bengal Gram in a small bowl for at least 10 minutes so as to soften it. Heat oil in a frying pan and add Cumin & Mustard seeds and Curry leaves. When crackling sound of seeds is heard, add Green Chillies and Ginger and wait for a minute, then add Tomato, Brinjal and Potato, water and lastly soaked Bengal Gram and stir well so as to blend all vegetables & spices. After cooking for a few minutes, remove the lid. Further cook the ingredients till the vegetables and Bengal Gram are softened. This dish is a good combination with Rotis or Chapathis.

# Spicy Pulse Curry

**Ingredients**

| | | | |
|---|---|---|---|
| Split Green Gram Dal | 2 cups | Garlic chopped | 1 tsp |
| Any one leafy vegetable | 2 cups | Red Chilly powder | 1 tsp |
| Turmeric powder | 1 tsp | Tomatoes | 1 no. |
| Salt | To taste | Cumin & Mustard seeds | 1 tsp |
| Ginger | 1 tsp | | |

**Process of preparation**

Chop leafy vegetable (choose either spinach or amaranthus or kenaf leave), after washing them. Slice the tomatoes and set aside, wash green gram lentils twice and boil in a pressure cooker for few minutes. Heat oil in a frying pan, then add chopped ginger, chopped garlic and sauté for a minute. Add Tomato slices, Turmeric and Chilly powder and stir it properly. There after add finely chopped leafy vegetable as well as boiled Green Gram and add one cup of water and blend all ingredients thoroughly so that the spices are mixed properly with vegetables. Let the ingredients cook on slow flame. Heat oil in another pan add cumin and mustard seeds to the oil and wait till the seeds sputter. Now pour all the cooked vegetables and spices mixture in the seasoned oil, stir well and remove from stove after garnishing with chopped coriander leaves.

## THOTAKURA (AMARANTHUS LEAVES) AND IT'S BENEFITS

There are different types of Amaranthus leaves or Thotakura viz Erra (Red) Thotakura, Koyya Thotakura, Perugu (Curd) Thotakura and Chiluka (Split) Thotakura.

This leafy vegetable is a salutary diet required for those have excessive body heat or urinary tract disease, It is useful for people suffering from wind. However, those suffering from Rheumatism or gout are advised to avoid this leafy vegetable. Chiluka Thotakura is known for curing all diseases and to cure infections and it also purifies blood. It increases our appetite and keeps our body fit and healthy.

# Thotakura (Amaranthus) Fry

**Ingredients**

| | | | |
|---|---|---|---|
| Thotakura leaves | 3 cups | Salt | To taste |
| Garlic | 4 pods | Green Chillis | 4 nos. |
| Cooking oil | 1 tsp | Black Gram Lentils | 1/4 tsp |
| Red Chilly powder | 1 tsp | Curry leaves | A few sprigs |
| Cumin Mustard seeds | As required | Red Chillies | 4 nos. |
| Turmeric | 1/4 tsp | Coriander Leaves | A few twigs |
| Onion | 1 no. | | |

**Process of preparation**

Clean amaranthus leaves in water well and chop the leaves along with tender stems into small pieces and set aside. Take a frying pan, pour oil in it. Heat it, and put Cumin and Mustard seeds along with Curry leaves and season the oil. Next add Red Chillies, Black Gram, Lentils and then after a while when Chillies and Black Gram also crackle, add chopped Thotakura leaves, Onion (chopped) and Green Chillies, Salt and Turmeric and stir the ingredients thoroughly. Add crushed Garlic, Salt, and Red Chilly powder. Before removing from stove, sprinkle chopped Coriander leaves.

# Thotakura Dal (Amaranthus with Lentils)

**Ingredients**

| | | | |
|---|---|---|---|
| Chopped Thotakura | 3 cups | Salt | To taste |
| Red Chilly Powder | 1 tsp | Cumin & Mustard seeds | As required |
| Red gram / Green gram | 1 cup | Black Gram seeds | 1 tsp |
| Turmeric powder | 1/4 tsp | Onion (sliced) | 1 no. |
| Cooking Oil | 1 tsp | Green Chillies (Chopped) | 4 nos. |

**Process of preparation**

Clean the Amaranthus (Thotakura) leaves in water and chop the leaves and tender stems and set aside. Heat oil in a frying pan add cumin & Mustard seeds and curry leaves for seasoning then, add onion and green chilly, sauté the ingredients for a while and then add chopped Amaranthus leaves and dhal and transfer all these into a pressure cooker. Add glass of water to the ingredients and let them boil till you hear 2 whistles of cooker. Remove the cooker from stove and gently grind the semisoft lentils with a wooden crusher or electric blender, to make paste of the pulses and leaves, add salt and let the contents simmer for a while and finally garnish with chopped coriander. This Dal/lentils is very nutritious for our health and suitable with rice.

# Thotakura (Amaranthus) Sour Curry

**Ingredients**

| | | | |
|---|---|---|---|
| Thotakura (chopped) | 3 cups | Cumin & Mustard | As required |
| Tomato (Sliced) | 1 cup | Onion (Sliced) | 1 no. |
| Red Chilly Powder | 1 tsp | Green Chillies (Chopped) | 3 nos. |
| Turmeric | 1/4 tsp | Curry leaves | As required |
| Salt | To taste | Coriander leaves | As required |
| Tamarind | Lime sized | | |

**Process of preparation**

Clean the Amaranthus (Thotakura) leaves and chop the leaves and also edible soft stems and set aside. Slice tomatoes Onion and Green Chillies also. Put some water in a pressure cooker, add, Amaranthus (chopped) leaves, Tomato slices, Onion slices, Green Chilly pieces, Red Chilly powder, Turmeric powder, Tamarind one after and the other, to the boiling water and allow the ingredients to boil for a few minutes till you hear 3 whistles of pressure or till the leaves and tomatoes have been totally cooked, whichever is earlier. Heat oil in a pan add Cumin and Mustard seeds and Curry leaves and when the seed start crackling, transfer the cooked Amaranthus curry into the seasoned oil, add Salt to it, stir and remove it from the stove. Amaranthus sour curry  is more compatible with rice.

This leafy vegetable curry helps in curing Tumour, Diabetes, and Heart Diseases as well. It helps us to have pleasant mood. It also cures constipation, It helps reduce overheating or high temperature of our body. These small leaves if consumed in curries is highly beneficial for our body.

# Sorel Leaves (Chukka Kura) - Dal

**Ingredients**

| | | | |
|---|---|---|---|
| Chukkakura | 2 cups | Onion (sliced) | 1 no. |
| Red Chilly Powder | 1 tsp | Green Chillies | 3 nos. |
| Turmeric | 1/4 tsp | Curry leaves | A few sprigs |
| Red Gram/Green Gram | 1 cup ful | Coriander leaves | a few twigs |
| Salt | To taste | Cumin & Mustard seeds | as required |
| Cooking Oil | 1 tbsp | | |

**Process of preparation**

Wash and chop onion, green chillies, coriander leaves and keep them in separate bowls. Also wash Red Gram/Green Gram Lentils thoroughly in water.

Take some water in a pressure cooker, add Red Gram / Green Gram Lentils, chopped greens, sliced Onion, chopped Green Chillies, Turmeric and Red chilly powder to the water and boil till 3 whistles of the cooker. Then open the lid of the cooker and mash the leaves with a wooden masher, or electric blender and add salt to taste. Heat oil in a frying pan and add seasoning ingredients, When seeds start cracking, add the cooked leaves, Lentils to the seasoned oil and then keep it on slow flame for a few minutes and finally before removing from stove garnish with chopped Coriander leaves. This Dal is very nutritious, good for our health and tasty as well.

# Chukka Kura - Senaga Pappu (Split Bengal Gram) Curry

**Ingredients**

| | | | |
|---|---|---|---|
| Chukka leaves Chopped | 3 cups | Cooking Oil | 2 tbsps |
| Curry leaves | A few sprigs | Turmeric | 1/4 tsp |
| Split Bengal Gram (soaked) | 1 cup | Cumin & Mustard Seeds | As required |
| Coriander leaves | A few twigs | Salt | To taste |
| Onion chopped | 1 no. | Green Chillies (Chopped) | 4 nos. |
| Red Chilly Powder | 1 tsp | Ginger Chopped | 4 pieces |

**Process of preparation**

Wash and chop chukka leaves. Soak Bengal Gram in water & chop Chillies and Coriander leaves and set aside. Add soaked Bengal gram, chopped chukka leaves, chopped onion, chopped Green Chillies, chopped Ginger pieces with sufficient water to a pressure cooker, and let the ingredients boil for a few minutes till you hear 2 whistles of cooker. Heat oil in a frying pan and add Cumin & Mustard seeds and Curry leaves to the Oil and when seeds splutter add ingredients from the pressure cooker into the frying pan for seasoning. Finally, garnish the curry with chopped coriander, before removing from the stove.

# Sorel (Chukka Kura) Pachadi

**Ingredients**

| | | | |
|---|---|---|---|
| Chukka leaves | 3 cups | Mustard seeds powder | 1 tsp |
| Garlic Crushed | 6 pods | Red Chilly Powder | 1 tsp |
| Cooking oil | 2 tsp | Tamarind pulp | 1 tsp |
| Salt | To taste | Turmeric Powder | 1/4 tsp |
| Cumin Seeds powder | ½ tsp | Green Chillies (Chopped) | A few twigs |
| Cumin (cluster) | As required | Coriander leaves | A few twigs |

**Process of preparation:** Heat oil in a frying pan, add chopped green Chillies and chukka leaves to it and cook till the leaves curry into soft gravy. Chop Coriander leaves, crush peeled Garlic. Mix cooked leaves, garlic, Cumin and Mustard Seeds powder, Green Chillies and grind all of these into a fine paste. Take a thick vessel, pour oil and keep it on stove and season the oil with seasoning (mustard and cumin) seeds. Add salt and Turmeric powders and transfer the ground paste into the vessel and blend all the ingredients and finally garnish the chukka leaves chutney with chopped coriander and serve. This chutney is a good combination with rice. We can if so desire, use dry Red Chillies instead of Green Chillies. It will add to the taste.

## 2nd Variant of the Curry

In a pan heat and season the oil with Cumin and Mustard seeds as well as Curry leaves then add soaked Bengal Gram, chopped Green Chillies, stir all ingredients well and let them sauté for a few minutes and when these are half cooked, add Chukka kura leaves and finally add Salt, Chilly Powder, Turmeric and allow all the ingredients to cook for 2 more minutes, finally garnish the curry with chopped coriander leaves and serve. This recipe is very tasty, especially in combination with non-vegetarian items.

# Fenugreek (Methi) Leaves

## Fenugreek Leaves - Paneer (Methi Paneer)

**Ingredients**

| | | | |
|---|---|---|---|
| Paneer 250 gms | Chopped | Fenugreek | 2 cups |
| Coriander leaves | A few twigs | Garam Masala | ½ tsp |
| Tomatoes | 2 or 3 | Salt | To taste |
| Cooking oil | 2 tbsps | Green Chillies | 3 nos. |
| Ginger Garlic paste | 1 tsp | | |

**Process of preparation**

Cut paneer into pieces of desired size or cubes. chop Chillies, slice Tomatoes, and set aside. Heat oil in a pan and add Green Chillis, Ginger Garlic paste, followed by Fenugreek (Methi) leaves and fry all of these. After a minute, add Tomatoes and then Paneer pieces/cubes to it, and stir well. Let the ingredients cook for 5 minutes till the paneer cubes become soft and gravy is formed. Before removing from stove, add garam masala powder and chopped coriander leaves for garnishing.

## Fenugreek Leaves - Split Bengal Gram

**Ingredients**

| | | | |
|---|---|---|---|
| Chopped Fenugreek leaves | 3 cups | Coriander leaves | A few twigs |
| Ginger Garlic | little bit | Cumin seeds | 1/4th tsp |
| Split Bengal Gram | 1 cup | Curry leaves | A few sprigs |
| Red Chilly powder | 1 tsp | Mustard seeds | 1/4 tsp |
| Cooking Oil | 1 tsp | Fenugreek | 1/4 tsp |
| Salt | 1 tsp | Black Gram | ½ cup |
| Onion | Big sized | Green Chillies | 4 nos. |
| Turmeric Powder | 1/4 tsp | Red Chilly | 1 No. |

**Process of preparation**

Chop the fenugreek leaves, Onion and Green Chillies and set aside separately. Heat oil in a pan and add Cumin and Mustard seeds to it, and when seeds splutter, add Onion, Chillies, Ginger-Garlic paste, Split Bengal gram, Fenugreek leaves, Salt, Turmeric and Chilly powder and water and stir the ingredients. Its optional to add sliced tomatoes. Finally garnish the curry with chopped coriander.

# Fenugreek Lentils (Menthikura - Dal)

## Ingredients

| | |
|---|---|
| Chopped Fenugreek leaves | 3 cups |
| Coriander leaves | 2 twigs |
| Red Chilly Powder | 1 tsp |
| Cumin seeds | 1/4 tsp |
| Red Gram | 1 cup |
| Mustard seeds | 1/4 tsp |
| Garam Masala | 1 tsp |
| Fenugreek seeds | 1/4 tsp |
| Salt | To taste |
| Red Dry Chilly powder | 1tsp |
| Onion (chopped Big size) | 1 no. |
| Black Gram | ½ tsp |
| Turmeric powder | 1/4 tsp |
| Green Chillies | 2 nos. |
| Tamarind | Lime sized |
| Curry leaves | 2 sprigs |

**Process of preparation**

Wash and chop fenugreek leaves. Wash the red gram/green gram lentils. Boil the lentils in a pressure cooker. When the lentils are half cooked, add chopped fenugreek leaves, chopped onions, Green Chillies, Ginger, Red Chilly Powder, Turmeric and tamarind to the boiling lentils and wait till three whistles of the cooker. Now after the pressure is reduced open the lid of the cooker and soften the lentils with wooden masher and add Salt. Heat oil in a pan and add Cumin and Mustard seeds, Fenugreek seeds, Dry Chilly and Black Gram to the hot oil and when the seeds start crackling add this to the boiled lentils and garnish with chopped coriander leaves. This dish is very tasty and healthy since fenugreek leaves & seeds, both have medicinal value and lentils give proteins to our body.

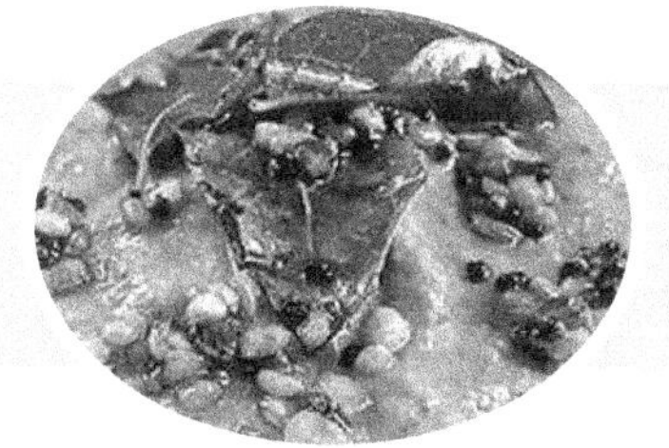

# Fenugreek Chutney

## Ingredients

| | |
|---|---|
| Fenugreek leaves | 3 cups |
| Gingelly Seeds | 1/4 tsp |
| Dry Red Chillies | 6-8 nos. |
| Coriander leaves | 2 twigs |
| Cooking Oil | 1 tbsp |
| Coriander seeds | 1 tsp |
| Garlic (Peeled & Crushed) | 2 nos. |
| Cumin Seeds | 1/4 tsp |
| Onion (Big) Sliced | 1 no. |
| Mustard Seeds | 1/4 tsp |
| Turmeric Powder | 1/4 tsp |
| Fenugreek Seeds | ½ tsp |
| Green Chillies (Chop) | 2 nos. |
| Red Chilly | 1 no. |
| Salt | To taste |
| Black Gram | ½ tsp |
| Curry leaves | 2 sprigs |
| Tamarind | Lime sized |

**Process of preparation:** Wash and chop fenugreek leaves. Heat oil in a pan, then add 6-8 dry chillies, 1 tsp coriander seeds, few Fenugreek seeds, 1/4th sesame (gingelly) seeds and roast these in oil and prepare fine powder by grinding in a mixer and keep aside. The next step is to take some water in a bowl, add tamarind to it and warm it slightly. After a while, remove the bowl from the stove, allow it to cool and add crushed garlic, fenugreek leaves, roasted spice powder and tamarind. Take another frying pan, pour oil in it, and when heated add cumin & mustard seeds, fenugreek seeds, red (dry) chillies and black gram to the oil for Seasoning roasted spice and crushed garlic to the seasoned oil, stir the contents and remove the pan from stove. Similarly we can prepare chutney of any other leafy vegetables roast the spices and add it to the paste of the leaf as mentioned above, blend both and season the mixture together. This chutney can be preserved for one month.

# Kenaf Leaves

Kenaf leaves are a very popular leafy vegetable in Telugu states and are very nutritious. These leaves have the qualities of strengthening our liver . Kenaf leaves, if dried, powdered, and tied in a cloth and applied on ulcers, ulcers vanish in no time. The Curry/ Chutney made from these leaves also enhances our appetite.

## Kenaf Leaves - Lentils (Gongura Pappu)

**Ingredients**

| | | | |
|---|---|---|---|
| Kenaf leaves (chopped) | 2 cups | Cumin & Mustard seeds | As required |
| Curry leaves | 4 sprigs | Salt | To taste |
| Red Gram Dal | 1 cup | Onion (sliced) | 1 no. |
| Coriander leaves | as required | Tamarind | Lime sized |
| Cooking oil | 2 tbsps | Green Chillis (chopped) | 4 Nos. |
| Red Chilly Powder | 1 tbsps | | |

**Process of preparation**

Wash, chop and then boil the  kenaf leaves in sufficient water in a pressure cooker. Clean and wash Red Gram Lentils, and add to the kenaf leaves, next add chopped onion, chopped Green Chillies, little bit of Tamarind, Red Chilly powder, Turmeric powder and Salt and½ cup of water. Blend well by stirring. Cook all these ingredients till you hear 3 whistles of the pressure cooker. Remove the lid of the cooker and mash the lentils and the kenaf leaves  with wooden masher or electric blender.

Take a frying pan, heat the oil in it, and cumin & mustard seeds and curry leaves for seasoning. Add the seasoned oil to the pre-boiled kenaf leaves lentils mixture, garnish with chopped coriander leaves and remove from stove.

Note: It is to be noted that kenaf leaves lentils require little bit of more salt when compared to other leafy vegetables at the same time, these leaves are highly beneficial for our health.

## Kenaf Leaves Green Chillies Chutney

**Ingredients**

| | | | |
|---|---|---|---|
| Chopped Kenaf leaves | 2 cups | Tamarind | Lime sized |
| Garlic | 6 pods | Green Chillies | 6-8 nos. |
| Cooking oil | 2 tbsps | Cumin & Mustard | As required |
| Salt | To taste | Curry leaves | 4 sprigs |
| Onion | 1 no. | Coriander leaves | 4 twigs |

**Process of preparation**

Clean Kenaf leaves in water, chop the leaves, and boil in a pressure cooker along with Tamarind and sufficient water. Add chopped Green Chillies, Salt and Garlic and Grind all the ingredients.

Take some oil in a frying pan heat it sufficiently and add  cumin and mustard seed along with curry leaves and once the seeds splutter, add the seasoned oil to the pre-cooked kenaf leaves mixture.

# Palak (Spinach)

- ✓ Aids detoxification
- ✓ Weight management
- ✓ Lowers blood pressure
- ✓ Improves digestion
- ✓ Improves skin and eyes
- ✓ Prevents cancer
- ✓ Reduces inflammation
- ✓ Healthy hear & etc.

## Palak Paneer (Spinach Paneer) Curry

**Ingredients**

| | | | |
|---|---|---|---|
| Spinach Chopped | 4 cups | Ginger-Garlic paste | 1 tsp |
| Coriander powder | 1 tsp | Garam Masala | 1 tsp |
| Paneer cubes | ½ cup | Coriander Chopped | a few twigs |
| Turmeric powder | 1/4 tsp | Salt | to taste |
| Onion sliced | ½ cup | Green Chillies (pieces) | 2-3 nos. |
| Red Chilly Powder | 1 tsp | Cooking oil | As required |

**Process of preparation**

Boil spinach and grind to a puree in a mixer. Heat oil in a pan add sliced onion pieces till they change color to red/ brown. Now add the ginger garlic paste ,Green Chillies and fry along with onion for a while and add boiled coarsely ground spinach, coriander powder, garam masala powder stir all the ingredients so as to blend them well. When the ingredients are half cooked, add paneer pieces to the cooked spinach, and let it Simmer for a few more minutes till the paneer cubes are cooked and absorb pieces and blends well with spinach. Finally, when the curry is done Garnish with chopped coriander leaves and remove the pan from the stove.

This is very popular and tasty curry and can be accompanied with both rice as well as Chapathis.

## Palak Mutter (Spinach-Peas) Curry

**Ingredients**

| | | | |
|---|---|---|---|
| Chopped Spinach | 2 cups | Asafoetida | 1/4 tsp |
| Boiled Peas | ½ cup | Red Chillies | 2 nos. |
| Cooking Oil | 2 tbsps | Turmeric Powder | 1/4 tsp |
| Milk | ½ cup | Salt | to taste |
| Cinnamon | ½ inch piece | Dried Ginger | 1 tsp |

**Process of preparation**

Clean, chop and boil the  Spinach in 5 cups of water, in a pressure cooker. While boiling Spinach, add peas and boil both for about 10 to 12 minutes or till entire water evaporates, add Chilly Powder, Turmeric Powder, dried Ginger, Milk and finally Salt, and stir all ingredients thoroughly to facilitate quick blending.

Keep a frying pan over lighted stove, heat oil in it, when properly heated add cloves and cinnamon to the oil, roast them for a while and add boiled spinach and peas mixture to this oil. This curry is very popular especially in north India, and is very tasty curry and should preferably be eaten while it is hot.

# Spinach - Bengal Gram Curry

**Ingredients**

| | | | |
|---|---|---|---|
| Spinach (Chopped) | 3 cups | Green Chillies (Chopped) | 5 nos. |
| Split Bengal Gram | 1 cup | Curry Leaves | a few sprigs |
| Cumin & Mustard Seeds | as required | Coriander leaves | a few twigs |
| Onion (Sliced) | 1 no. | Cooking Oil | 1 tsp. |

**Process of preparation**

Clean and chop spinach. Soak split Bengal Gram in water one hour in advance (before cooking) in order to make it soft. Heat oil in a pan, add Cumin and Mustard Seeds and Curry leaves for seasoning. When seeds start spluttering, add chopped Onions and Chilly pieces to the seasoned Oil and wait till Onion pieces become red/brown. Now, add soaked Bengal Gram and add water to cook it when it is half - cooked. Add chopped Spinach, followed by Salt, Chilly Powder, Turmeric Powder. After a few minutes of cooking, when the Bengal Gram is completely cooked and becomes soft, remove the pan from the stove and Garnish Curry with Chopped Coriander. This Tasty recipe is compatible with both rice as well as Chapathis.

# Spinach-Tomato Sour Curry

**Ingredients**

| | | | |
|---|---|---|---|
| Spinach ) | 3 cups | Coriander Leaves | a few twigs |
| Tomatoes (sliced) | 1 cup | Red Chilly Powder | 1 tsp |
| Onions (sliced) | 1 Big | Salt | to taste |
| Green Chillies | 4 nos. | Tamarind | little bit |
| Curry Leaves | a few sprigs | | |

**Process of preparation**

Clean and chop spinach leaves. Slice tomatoes, and boil both Spinach and tomato pieces in a cooker with sufficient water. Later add sliced Onion, Green Chilly pieces. Tamarind (optional), Salt, Chilly Powder and Turmeric Powder. Allow all the ingredients to boil vigorously for a while.

Heat oil in a pan, add Cumin and Mustard seeds and Curry leaves to it. When the seeds start crackling, add the pre-cooked Spinach, tomato mixture, to the seasoned Oil and stir well so that the oil is mixed uniformly in the entire Curry. In the end garnish the sour Curry with Chopped Coriander before removing from the stove.

# Spinach-Lentil (Palakura-Pappu)

**Ingredients**

| | | | |
|---|---|---|---|
| Spinach (chopped) | 3 cups | Green Chillies | 4 nos. |
| Split Red or Split Green Gram | 1 cup | Coriander leaves | a few twigs |
| Cooking Oil | 1 tbsp | Red Chilly Powder | 2 tsp |
| Cumin & Mustard Seeds | as required | Salt | to taste |
| Onion (sliced) | 1 no. | Turmeric Powder | 1/4 tsp |
| Curry Leaves | a few sprigs | Tamarind | little bit |

**Process of preparation**

Clean the Spinach leaves (in clear water twice, rearrange into bunch and chop), clean the split Red Gram or split Green Gram (as per your choice) in water twice and set aside. Slice Onion, chop few Green Chillies and set aside. Take some water in a pressure cooker, add split Bengal Gram to it, add the chopped Spinach, Onions, Green Chillis, Tamarind, Chilly powder and Turmeric powder, to the water. Cook all the ingredients in a pressure cooker for about 3 whistles, when the pressure of the cooker subsides, remove it's lid and soften the Red Gram or Green Gram with a wooden masher. Now add salt to the boiled ingredients and stir.

Heat oil in a frying pan then add Cumin & Mustard seeds and Curry Leaves and once the seeds crackle pour the boiled Red Gram-Spinach mixture into the pan and garnish with freshly chopped Coriander Leaves and serve.

This recipe is most commonly used one in Telugu states especially and is a tasty preparation, suitable with the combination of rice.

# Spinach Chutney

**Ingredients**

| | | | |
|---|---|---|---|
| Spinach (chopped) | 3 cups | Coriander | a few twigs |
| Cooking Oil | 2 tbsps | Garlic (peeled and chopped) | 4 pods |
| Cumin & Mustard seeds | as required | Sesame seeds | 3 tsps |
| Green Chillies (chopped) | 8-10 | Turmeric powder | 1/4 tsp |
| Curry Leaves | a few sprigs | Coriander powder | 3 tsps |

**Process of preparation**

Wash and chop spinach. Keep a pan on lighted stove, pour some Oil, heat it up, add chopped Green Chillies and chopped Spinach to it and let it cook in the Oil for a few minutes.

In another pan, roast fenugreek seeds, Cumin seeds and Coriander seeds, and grind altogether in a mixer and keep it in a separate bowl.

Now, put cooked Spinach, Green Chillies & Tamarind in a mixer and add Coriander powder, Cumin Powder & Fenugreek powder, powdered Sesame, peeled and crushed Garlic pods to it and grind all the ingredients together. Finally add this ground Spinach & Spices mixture to the Seasoned Oil and garnish with chopped Coriander.

Spinach Chutney is very nutritious. The Calcium inherent in sesame seeds and the fiber and Vitamins available in Spinach, help strengthen our bones.

# Sour Curries

## Horsegram Sour Curry (Ulava Charu)

**Ingredients**

| | | | |
|---|---|---|---|
| Horse Gram | 500 gms. | Curry leaves | a few sprigs |
| Water | 2 liters | Coriander leaves | a few twigs |
| Cooking oil | 2 tbsps | Red Chilly Powder | 2 tsps |
| Cumin & Mustard seeds | as required | Turmeric Powder | 1/4 tsp |
| Onion (chopped) | 2 nos. | Salt | to taste |
| Green Chillies | 3-4 nos. | Tamarind | little bit |

**Process of preparation:** Pour 2 liters of water in a pressure cooker and add Horse Gram (cleaned in water) and keep it on a lighted stove and boil till you hear 12-13 whistles. When the cooker is removed from the stove, and its pressure subsides, filter the Ingredients and transfer the residual water to a bowl. Add Salt, Chilly powder, Turmeric Powder and Tamarind to the residual Horse Gram soup and boil it again in the pressure cooker. After a few minutes of intense boiling, when the ingredients form a thick/dense gravy like spicy soup, remove from stove. In another frying pan, kept on lighted stove, pour Oil, and after it is heated sufficiently, add Cumin &Mustard seeds and Curry Leaves. When the seeds start spluttering,  add the Horse Gram sour Soup to the seasoned Oil and finally garnish the liquid with chopped Coriander. This is a very tasty and popular preparation of Telugu states, and also compatible with rice.

**Note:** Those interested can add drumstick pieces, and boiled eggs to this dish.

## Kenaf Leaves - Split Bengal gram Sour Curry

**Ingredients**

| | | | |
|---|---|---|---|
| Kenaf leaves | 2 cups | Red Chilly powder | ½ tsp |
| Split Bengal Gram | ½ cup | Turmeric Powder | 1 tsp |
| Cooking Oil | 1 tbsp | Salt | to taste |
| Tamarind (soaked) | little bit | Cumin & Mustard seeds | as required |
| Onion (sliced) | 2 nos. | Coriander leaves | a few twigs |
| Green Chillies | 4 nos. | Curry Leaves | a few sprigs |
| Garlic (peeled & crushed) | 4 pods | | |

**Process of preparation:** Clean and chop kenaf leaves. Clean the Bengal Gram in water and soak it in water for some time. Soak Tamarind for at least 2 hrs before cooking. Squeeze it afterwards and prepare its pulp and set aside. Slice Onions, chop Green Chillies, coriander leaves and peel and crush garlic. Take some water in a pressure cooker and add cleaned and chopped Kenaf leaves, soaked Split Bengal Gram, sliced onions and Green Chillies, Chilly powder, Turmeric and lastly Salt in that order. Boil all ingredients together till 3 whistles of cooker are heard and ingredients are cooked properly. Heat oil in a frying pan, add Cumin & Mustard seeds and Curry leaves to the hot oil. To this add the boiled Kenaf leaves-Bengal Gram mixture and garnish with chopped Coriander before serving hot.

**2nd Variant:** Firstly, boil Kenaf leaves, then season the Oil with Cumin & Mustard seeds and Curry Leaves, then add  Bengal Gram, Sliced Onion, Chopped Green Chillies, Tamarind, Chilly powder, Turmeric and boil all the ingredients. Lastly add boiled Kenaf leaves, Salt to taste in the end since Kenaf leaves and a few other leafy vegetables do not cook quickly if salt added to it initially.

# Rice Items

# Veg. Pulav

## Ingredients

| | | | |
|---|---|---|---|
| Basmathi Rice | 1 cup | Medium Potato | 1 no. (diced) |
| French Beans | 6 nos. (cut into pieces) | Medium Carrot | 1 no. (diced) |
| Cauliflowers florets | 8 to 10 | Large Tomato (grated) | 1 no. |
| Shelled Peas | ½ cup | Green Chillies | 3 nos. |
| Onion | 1 no. (sliced) | Garlic Paste | ½ tsp |
| Cinnamon stick | 1" | Cloves | 3 nos. |
| Green Cardamoms | 2 nos. | Coriander + mint leaves | 5+5 |
| Water | 2 cups | Salt | to taste |

**Spice powders:**

| | | | |
|---|---|---|---|
| Chilly powder | ½ tsp. | Turmeric powder | ¼ tsp |
| Garam Masala Powder | 1 tsp. | | |

**Seasoning**

| | | | |
|---|---|---|---|
| Onion | 1 no. sliced | Oil / Ghee | 1 to 2 tsp. |

**Process of preparation:** Pre-heat the pan, pour oil or ghee, add the whole spices and the onions, cover and cook for 4 minutes on low heat till the onions turn light brown, add the ginger garlic paste and spice powders. Stir in the tomato and vegetables, cover and cook.

Now add the rice, add the water, green chillies, coriander and mint leaves and salt, stir in the tomato and vegetables, cover and cook on low heat for 18 to 20 minutes till the rice is done. Remove from the heat and keep the seasoning covered for a few more minutes Pre-heat the pan, add the ghee and onions, fry the onions till golden brown. Turn off the heat and mix into the pulav. Serve hot with a raitha of your choice.

# Bisi Bela Bath

**Ingredients**

| | | | |
|---|---|---|---|
| Basmathi Rice | ½ kg | Cashew nuts | 10-15 pieces |
| Red gram (Split) | 300 gm | Mustard seeds | 1 tsp |
| Tamarind (Soaked) | 50 gm | Garlic (peeled chopped) | 1 pod |
| Salt | To taste | Onion (chopped) | 2 nos. |
| Turmeric | 1/4 tsp | Black pepper seeds | 1½ tsp |
| Cooking oil | 1 cup | Jaggery | 1 tsp |
| Butter / Ghee | 1 cup | Cumin seeds | 1 tsp |
| Raw Dry coconut | 50 gms | Cashew nuts | 6 nos. |
| **Vegetables** | | Potatoes | 2 nos. |
| Carrot | 100 gm | Beans | 50 gm |
| Double Beans | 50 gm | Capsicum | 1 no. |

**Process of preparation:** Roast all ingredients required for preparing the Bisbela Masala (spice powder) viz Red Chilly flakes, coriander seeds, split Black Gram, Poppy seeds, Bengal gram, cinnamon, cloves, cumin seeds ,fenugreek seeds, mustard seeds, and black pepper seeds for sometime, and powder them finely in a grinder and keep aside in a small bowl. Put all vegetables peas, carrot pieces, Beans pieces, Double Beans pieces, capsicum pieces and if desired - potato pieces in a pressure cooker add water to it and boil  till two whistles of  pressure cooker. Add rice, red gram and cook for further 2 or 3 whistles.  Heat oil in a pan, add cumin and mustard seeds, fenugreek seeds, and also black pepper seeds, once the seeds start spluttering , then add asafoetida (little bit), finely powdered spices, onion, Green Chillies stir all ingredients, add pre-boiled vegetables and let it cook for a while. Now add salt, turmeric, tamarind, pulp, red Chilly powder, mix all the ingredients once again, followed by cooked rice, split red gram and one cup of water . Once the  ingredients are cooked properly, garnish the Bisibela Bath with chopped coriander before removing from the stove.

This recipe is very tasty as well as it is very good for health since it consists of various nutritious vegetables, lentils and spices etc.

# Vaangi Bath

**Ingredients**

| | | | |
|---|---|---|---|
| Rice | 3 glasses | Coriander seeds | 3 tsp |
| Cooking oil | 1/4 cup | Mustard Seeds | 1 tsp |
| Brinjal | 1/4 kg | Dry Chillies | 6 nos. |
| Onion | 1 no | Turmeric powder | ½ tsp |
| Split Black gram | 3 tsp | Cinnamon | 2" long-1 no. |
| Tamarind | Lime sized | Cloves | 4 nos. |
| Bengal gram | 3 tsps | Cardamom | 2 nos. |
| Cashew nuts | 10 pieces | Asafoetida | little bit |

**Process of preparation**

Roast all spices separately and grind them into fine powder in a rice cooker, cook rice and keep aside. Squeeze the tamarind already soaked in water and collect its pulp in a small bowl and set aside. Chop the onion into small pieces. Peel  the garlic  and  cut the brinjals into big pieces. Heat oil in a pan add mustard seeds and garlic pods, followed by cashew nuts, curry leaves, onion pieces, asafoetida, turmeric, and pieces of brinjals. Stir these ingredients well and keep the cooker on low flame. After the ingredients are cooked properly, add tamarind pulp followed by finally powdered spices. Add the cooked gravy to the cooked rice and stir properly so that all ingredients and spices spread evenly in the rice. Remove from stove, squeeze one lime and add its juice and sprinkle the chopped coriander over the rice. This is very tasty when it is hot.

## Tamarind Rice (Pulihora)

### Ingredients

| | | | |
|---|---|---|---|
| Rice | 1 kg | Split Black gram | 3 tsps |
| Cooking oil | 100 gm | Curry leaves | 10 twigs |
| Tamarind | 100 gm | Mustard seeds | 1 tsp |
| Red Chilly flakes | few | Turmeric | 1 tsp |
| Ginger (chopped) | 3 tsp | Groundnuts | 3 tsps |
| Split Bengal gram | 3 tsp | Salt | to taste |
| Green Chillies | 8 nos. | Cashew nuts | As desired |

### Process of preparation

Clean tamarind in water, soak it in water for one hour and squeeze its pulp (The pulp should be thick) boil it, and set aside. In a rice cooker, cook rice without allowing it to cook soft, spread the cooked rice in a tray, pour some oil in it without heating, add curry leave twigs (not leaves) turmeric, green chillies, ginger pieces and cover with a layer of cooked rice and leave it for 10 mins,  Heat oil in a pan, season it with dry Chillies, split Bengal gram, black gram, Mustard seeds, ground nuts, cashew nuts & curry leaves. Add tamarind pulp & salt to the seasoned oil. Remove the curry leaves from the rice and add the tamarind paste and mix well.

In other variants, dried chillies and coriander are roasted and powdered and added to rice. In some variants of Pulihora, mustard powder is mixed with rice. Hence, we can also prepare this recipe with some variations. This recipe is usually prepared on almost every festival or domestic functions or celebrations.

This is a favorite dish liked by everyone. This recipe can also be prepared by adding raw mango pulp and also with lime juice, instead of tamarind, along with other basic ingredients like oil, turmeric, green chillies, ginger, and curry leaves. In a novel method, we can also grind curry leaves and fry the paste and add to the rice. Another variety of pulihora is to use citrus/citron (Dabbakaya) juice, instead of tamarind pulp, or we can use Amla pieces, instead of tamarind.

# Kenaf Leaves Pulihora (Gongura Pulihora)

**Ingredients**

| | | | |
|---|---|---|---|
| Rice (cooked) | 3 cups | Cooking oil | As desired |
| Turmeric powder | 1 tsp | Groundnut | 3 tsps |
| Bengal gram | 1tsp | Black gram | 1 tsp |
| Kenaf leaves | 2 cups | Green Chillies | 6 nos. |
| Salt | to taste | Cashew nuts | if desired |
| Tamarind | little bit | Curry leaves | 5 nos. |

**Process of preparation**

Boil kenaf leaves to a paste like consistency and set aside. While the cooked rice is hot enough, add turmeric, green Chillies, ginger pieces, curry leaves, and 3 spoons of unheated oil and mix, all ingredients in the rice. In a small bowl, heat oil, add dry Chillis, Bengal gram, black gram , mustard seeds, cashew nuts, groundnuts. After the mustard splutters add tamarind pulp and kenaf paste and season in oil. Remove curry leaves from the seasoned oil within a minute of seasoning the oil. Mix cooked paste with rice along with salt and serve.

1. In another variant of Pulihora mustard powder is also used.

2. Pulihora can be prepared differently by roasting coriander seeds, dry chillies, cumin seeds together and grinding to powder and mixing the same in the rice.

# Green Pulav

**Ingredients**

| | | | |
|---|---|---|---|
| Rice  Cooked | 2 cups | Potatoes (Boiled) | 2 |
| Garam Masala | 1 tsp | Mint leaves | 1 big bunch |
| Ghee/Butter | 2 tsp | Water | As required |
| Onion (Finely chopped) | ½ cup | Green Chillies | 8 nos. |
| Raw peas | 1 cup | Salt | to taste |
| Coriander leaves | 1 big bunch | Ginger Garlic paste | 1 tsp |

**Process of preparation**

Take a thick pan or bowl, pour some ghee/ butter cooking oil and  heat it.  Add chopped onion and wait till the onion browns, add garam masala, ginger garlic paste, Coriander, leaves, mint leaves, and fry it. Add potato pieces and raw peas along with salt and cooked rice. Saute covered for some time and remove the pan / bowl from the stove. This dish is  to be eaten along with curd chutney.

# Jeera Rice

**Ingredients**

| | | | |
|---|---|---|---|
| Basmathi Rice | 1/4 kilogram | Ghee/butter / oil | 2 tsps |
| Cashew nuts | As required | Cloves | 4 nos. |
| Shah jeera (spice) | 1 tsp | Salt | to taste |
| Cumin seeds | 2 tsps | Cardamom | 4 nos. |

**Process of preparation**

Wash and soak rice for 30 minutes. Heat ghee/ oil in a pan  and add shah jeera , Cumin seeds, cloves and cardommon saute for1 min and add 2 cups of water to it. Let the water boil vigorously. Then add soaked and strained rice it and cook till rice is done. Can be garnished with browned or carmelized onions. Can serve with chicken curry.

# Coconut Rice

**Ingredients**

| | | | |
|---|---|---|---|
| Basmathi Rice | 1/2 kg | Coriander leaves | As required |
| Coconut | 1 no. | Salt | to taste |
| Onion | 4 nos. | | |

Mustard , cumin seeds, black gram and Bengal gram  (For seasoning)

**Process of preparation**

Wash Basmathi Rice and soak. Take a tender coconut and grind it to a paste and set aside. Keep a thick bowl on stove and add 2 big spoons/ladles full of ghee/ refined cooking oil in the bowl and when it is heated sufficiently, add mustard and cumin seeds, cashew nuts, little bit of Bengal gram and black gram to it. After the seeds splutter add chopped onion and saute. Then add Basmati Rice and double the quantity of water, salt and ground coconut paste and  simmer covered .Stir it two three times and after the rice is cooked, add chopped coriander to it before removing from the stove. This dish should be enjoyed while it is hot. It is a very tasty dish.

# Coconut Rice with Spice

**Ingredients**

| | | | |
|---|---|---|---|
| Basmathi Rice | 1/2 kg | Ghee/ Refined Oil | 1 tsp |
| Cashew-nuts | 10 pieces | Cinnamon | 2" long |
| Coconut | 1 no. | Salt | To taste |
| Coriander leaves | little bit | Cardamom | 4 nos. |
| Cloves | 5 nos. | | |

**Process of preparation**

Take a coconut with thick and hard kernel and grate. Add hot water to it and grind. Squeeze coconut milk from ground paste. Wash the rice and soak for 30 mins. Heat ghee/oil in a pan and add cloves, cardamom, cinnamon, cashew nuts and after frying all these together, add washed rice and coconut milk (If one glass of water is used 2 glasses of coconut milk are to be used), salt, and keep stirring it constantly for a little while and remove from stove, when rice is cooked.

# Dried Peas (Batana) Fried Rice

**Ingredients**

| | | | |
|---|---|---|---|
| Dried Peas | 1 cup | Shah-jeera | A little bit |
| Nutmeg | small piece | Green Chillies | 4 nos. |
| Rice | 2 cups | Salt | to taste |
| Ginger, garlic paste | 1 tsp | Cinnamon | 1 inch long |
| Cardamom | 1 not | Cooking oil or ghee | 4 tsp |
| Onion (chopped) | 2 nos. | Coriander leaves  (chopped) | 1/4  cup |
| Cloves | 3 nos. | | |

**Process of preparation**

Heat oil/ghee in a pan, add all spices, together with mint leaves, followed by chopped onions, green chilly, and ginger garlic paste and fry all ingredients.

 Later add rice (after cleaning in water & straining clods etc.) and then 4 cups of water, and salt. Transfer all these ingredients into a pressure cooker and allow it to cook till you hear 3 whistles of the cooker. Put off the stove, remove the cooker from it, and garnish with chopped coriander leaves, after the pressure in the cooker subsides.

# Cabbage Rice

**Ingredients**

| | | | |
|---|---|---|---|
| Rice | 2 cups | Cabbage | 1 cup |
| Black pepper powder | 1/2 tsp | Salt | to taste |
| Ghee | 2 cups | Coriander leaves | Little bit |
| Onion (chopped) | ½ cup | Capsicum chopped | ½ cup |

**Process of preparation**

First cook rice and keep aside. Take a pan, pour ghee in it and heat it. Once it is sufficiently heated, add chopped onion and fry it till it turn brownish. Later, add chopped cabbage, and capsicum pieces to the ghee and onion and fry. Add salt and pepper powder together with cooked rice, stir nicely and add a spoonful of chopped coriander leaves. This is a very tasty dish.

# Spinach - Corn Pulav

**Ingredients**

| | | | |
|---|---|---|---|
| Basmati Rice | As desired | Asafoetida | A pinch |
| Spinach | 2 cups | Corn kennels | ½ cup |
| Turmeric | A pinch off | Onion (chopped) | 1 no. |
| Boiled Spinach Puree | 1 cup | Dry Raw Mango Powder (Aamchur) | Little bit |
| Green Chillies | 2 nos. | Cooking oil | As required |
| Mustard Seeds | 1 tsp | Salt | to taste |

**Process of preparation**

Heat oil in a pan, add mustard seeds (and wait till the seeds crackle) green Chillies and chopped ginger to it and fry. Add  Asafoetida and continue frying. Now add the spinach puree and stir the ingredients and continue to cook the contents. Next  add pre-cooked rice, pre-boiled  corn kernels, dry mango powder (Aamchur powder) and Salt. Stir the contents thoroughly, keep it on stove for a while and serve hot and relish it.

# Potato - Mixed Rice

**Ingredients**

| | | | |
|---|---|---|---|
| Rice | 1 cup | Green Chillies (spilt) | 2-3 |
| Cardamom | 2 or 7 | Cumin Seeds | 1 tsp |
| Ghee or oil | 2 tsp | Water | 2 cups |
| Crystal Salt | 1tsp | Cinnamon | 1 inch long |
| Potato (big sized) | 1 no. | Coriander seeds | 1 tsp |
| Onion (chopped) | 2 nos. | | |

**Process of preparation**

Heat ghee or cooking oil in it and add cumin seeds, cinnamon pieces, Cardamom and stir it. Now add potato pieces, rice, salt, Green Chillies (split vertically) allow these ingredients to cook for some time then add water and cover the pan with a lid. Wait for all ingredients to sauté and garnish with chopped coriander before removing from the stove. (Instead of pan, if the fried ingredients are transferred into a pressure cooker and cooked after adding water in it, the contents will cook fully and will enhance the taste of the potato kichdi.

# Tomato Rice

**Ingredients**

| | | | |
|---|---|---|---|
| Tomatoes | 1/2 kg | Cumin Seeds | 1 tsp |
| Mint leaves | 15 leaves | Asatfoetida (if desired) | little bit |
| Basmati Rice | 1/2 kg | Salt | to taste |
| Coriander leaves | little bit | Garam Masala powder | 1/2 spoon |
| Cashew nuts | 10 nos. | Curry leaves | a few |
| Mirchi Powder | 1tsp | Mustard seeds | ½ tsp |
| Cloves | 5 nos. | Dry (Red) Chillies | 1 or 2 |
| Ghee | 2 tsp | Onion (chopped) | 1/2 |
| Green Chillies (Chop) | 4 nos. | | |

**Process of preparation**

Heat oil in a pan, add Chilly flakes, cumin seeds, mustard seeds, cashew nuts, cloves and a little bit of Asafoetida (optional). Once these are fried properly, the color will turn brownish, then add chopped onion and fry till the onion turns brownish, followed by green chillies and curry leaves and finally chopped tomatoes, garam masala powder and finally salt , allow all the ingredients to sauté nicely. Cool and grind to a paste. Add this paste as the basmati rice is cooking. Mix well and serve once rice is fully cooked. Garnish with coriander leaves before removing from stove.

This Tomato Rice a very good combination with either chicken curry or Mutton curry or curd chutney.

In a different way - we can also cook rice and then add ground tomato paste to cooked paste.

# Pongal

**Ingredients**

| | | | |
|---|---|---|---|
| Rice | 1 cup | Ghee/ Butter | 1 tsp |
| Cumin seeds | A few twigs | Black pepper seeds | 10 nos. |
| Green gram | 1 cup | Ginger (crushed) - Small pieces coarsely | |

**Process of preparation**

Dry roast green gram in a pan till a nice aroma comes. In a pressure cooker melt ghee/butter and add black pepper seeds, crushed ginger pieces, cumin seeds, rice and roasted green gram to it, pour 3-4 cups of water, and cook till 2 whistles of cooker are heard and then put off the stove. This  is a very tasty dish and can be relished with either coconut chutney or groundnut chutney.

# Rasam

## Rasam (South Indian Soup)

**Ingredients**

| | | | |
|---|---|---|---|
| Tamarind | equal to 1 lime | Onion (chopped) | ½ Onion |
| Red gram | 1 tbsp | Oil | 1 tsp |
| Coriander Powder | 1 tbsp | Cumin & Mustard | 1/4 tsp |
| Pepper Corn | 1/2 tsp | Turmeric | 1/4 tsp |
| Cumin powder | 1 tsp | Coriander leaves | A little bit |
| Curry leaves | 5 leaves | Fenugreek seeds | A little bit |
| Garlic | 5 pods | Asafoetida | A little bit |
| Tomato | 2 nos. | | |

**Process of preparation**

Wash Tamarind thoroughly, soak it in warm water for 10 minutes. Squeeze tamarind to get the pulp and keep it aside. Chop tomato into small pieces and keep aside. In a mixer, add Red gram coriander seeds, pepper corn, cumin and grind it into fine powder. Also add peeled and crushed garlic pods, curry leaves and keep the mixture aside. Heat oil in a pan and add cumin & mustard seeds, garlic pieces and after frying for some time, add Tomato pieces, already prepared spice powder and Tamarind pulp. Add salt and Turmeric to the soup, boil it till 3 boils. Sprinkle coriander leaves over the top and serve hot.

## Tomato Rasam (Tomato Sour Liquid)

**Ingredients**

| | | | |
|---|---|---|---|
| Tomato | 1/4 kg | Salt | As Required |
| Onion (chopped) | 1 no. | Oil | 1 tsp |
| Green Chillies (pieces) | 2 nos. | | |

**Process of preparation**

Take tomatoes in a pressure cooker and add water to it, and boil. After the tomatoes are boiled grind in a mixer and set aside. Heat oil in a heavy bottomed pan and add cumin seeds, mustard seed, curry leaves. Once the seeds splutter add chopped onion, green chillies, boiled and ground tomatoes, salt and turmeric, and wait till two boils and remove the pan from the stove and garnish the Tomato Rasam with chopped Coriander leaves.

# Sambar (Spiced Lentils Liquid Dal)

**Ingredients**

| | | | |
|---|---|---|---|
| Red gram | 1 cup | Tomatoes | 2 nos. |
| Cooking oil | 2 tsp | Coriander | few strands |
| Tamarind (Soaked in water) | Little bit | Ginger pieces | ½ tsp |
| Cumin & Mustard seeds | as required | Sambar powder | 2 tsp |
| Onion (chopped) | 2 nos. | Salt | To taste |
| Drumstick | 1 no. | Fenugreek seeds | Little bit |

**Process of preparation**

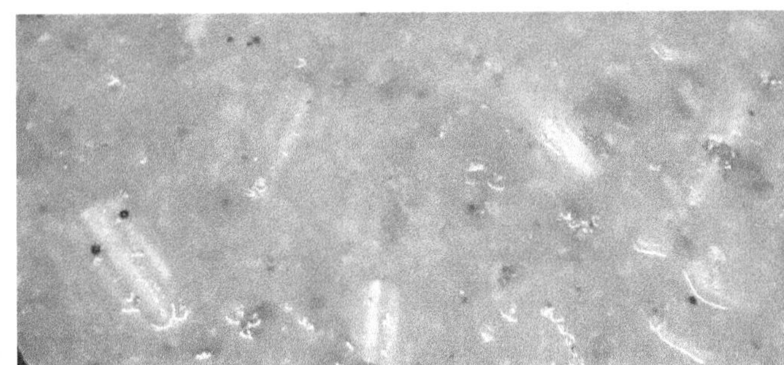

Wash and cook red gram with water in a pressure cooker till two whistles. Mash the cooked dal. Now, add drumstick cut into small pieces, tomato pieces, ginger, chopped green chillies, salt, red chilly powder, turmeric, Sambar powder (prepared by blending spices and red chilly powder), and finally tamarind pulp.

Cook the ingredients till the raw smell is gone and stir well. Remove from stove. Heat some oil in a small pan, add seasoning seeds viz. cumin and mustard seeds along with curry leaves. After the seeds splutter pour the cooked red gram dal into the seasoned oil and stir well so that the oil mixes evenly in the entire Dal and garnish with chopped coriander.

This recipe can also be prepared by using green gram dal, using Sambar powder, while using all ingredients as detailed above.

While preparing any sour liquid like Sambar the seasoning should be done only after everything is prepared and cooking process is completed.

# Green Gram Sour Liquid (Green Gram Rasam)

**Ingredients**

| | | | |
|---|---|---|---|
| Green gram | 1 glass | Seasoning seeds | As required |
| Onion (chopped into 4 pieces) | 1 no. | Curry leaves | 3 nos. |
| Green Chillies | 4 nos. | Coriander leaves | A little bit |
| Garlic | 3 pods | Cooking oil | 1 tsp |
| Lemon | 2 (Squeeze the juice out of it) | | |

**Process of preparation:** Take a pressure cooker, add green gram and roast it till the raw odor of the green gram vanishes. add chopped green Chillies and 2 glasses of water to it and cook till 2 whistles. After the pressure is released, soften the dal with a wooden cluster, then add onion pieces, 3 to 4 glasses of water followed by salt and turmeric and allow it to boil for 5 minutes after cooking is done, remove cooker from the stove and keep it aside. Now take another bowl or a pan, and pour oil in it after the oil is heated, add seasoning seeds, after the seeds start spluttering, add curry leaves, now pour the Rasam into the seasoned oil and stir the contents. Add lime juice, and remove the vessel, from the stove, garnish with coriander leaves. It gives coolness during summer. This dish can also be had as a snack along with Black gram (Vadiyaalu) (fried condiment vadiyaalu)

# Masala Rasam

**Process of preparation:** Oil 1 teaspoon, ghee 1 teaspoon, garam masala ½ teaspoon, fenugreek ½ teaspoon, mustard seed ½ teaspoon, black pepper 1 spoon, cumin seeds ½ teaspoon, small tomatoes 2 nos., onion and green chilly sliced and slit 2 nos. red chillis 2 nos. – all these should cook for 3 minutes. Add 20 gms. Tamarind juice, salt, turmeric ¼ teaspoon, coriander powder 1 teaspoon with all these cook for 5 minutes and add coriander, now it is ready.

## Sambar Powder

**Ingredients**

| | | | |
|---|---|---|---|
| Split black gram | 1 glass | Cumin seeds | 1 glass |
| Split bengal gram | 1 glass | Fenugreek seeds | ½ glass |
| Split green gram | 1 glass | Dry coconut (grated) | 1 glass |
| Split red gram | 1 glass | Rice | 2 tbsps |
| Coriander seeds | 3 glasses | | |

**Method of preparation:** Fry all the ingredients separately and powder them. Roast dry coconut in ghee and mix along with other powders in a mixer. Instead of dry coconut we can use 2 spoons of fresh grated coconut whenever preparing sambar.

## Garam Masala

**Ingredients**

| | | | |
|---|---|---|---|
| Coriander seeds | 750 g. | Cloves | 25 g. |
| Marati Mogga | 5 g. | Pepper | 25 g. |
| Garlic | 50 g. | Shazeera | 50 g. |
| Asafotida | 20 g. | Dry mirchi powder | 50 g. |
| Cinnamon stick | 25 g. | Cardamom | 25 g. |
| Nutmegs | 1 no. | Poppy seeds | 50 g. |
| Bay leaf | 25 g. | Javithri | 25 g. |
| Star anis | 25 g. | Sounf | 20 g. |
| Turmeric powder | 50 g or 25 g | Rice – roast till it is red | 50 g. |
| Salt | 50 g. (roast) | | |

**Method of preparation:** Fry coriander seeds and cumin till you get nice flavor, fry the other ingredients lightly and powder them. Mix all the powders and store them in a glass jar. Fry garlic in ghee and add to other powders, add salt and rice powder also. Store in a glass jar.

# Idli Powder

**Ingredients**

| | | | |
|---|---|---|---|
| Split bengal gram (fried) | ½ kilo | Dried coconut | 200 grams |
| Cumin | 50 grams | Salt | 60 grams |
| Garlic | 50 grams | Ghee | 100 grams |
| Red Chilly | 50 grams | | |

**Method of preparation**

Put fried chana dal, cumin, garlic, dried chilly in a mixer and powder. Grate the dried coconut. Powder the chana dal. Fry cumin seeds and powder it. Grind garlic and fry it in ghee till it turns red. Fry dry coconut in the same way. Later pulse chana dal powder, chilli powder, fried dry coconut, and fried garlic paste in a mixer. Store it in a container. It can be preserved up to a month.

# Black Chilli Powder (Nalla Karam)

**Ingredients**

| | | | |
|---|---|---|---|
| Red chilly (fried with a little oil) | 1 kilo | Gingelly/sesame seeds | 75 grams |
| Tamarind (cleaned by removing the fibres) | ½ kilo | Cumin seeds | 100 grams |
| Split bengal gram | 75 grams | Garlic | ½ kilo |
| Split black gram | 75 grams | Salt | ½ kilo |
| Poppy seeds | 75 grams | Sesame oil | 500 gms |

**Method of preparation**

Fry and powder split bengal gram, split black gram, sesame seeds, poppy seeds, cumin seeds separately till they turn red and smell good. In a bowl, mix coriander seeds powder, chilli powder, split bengal gram and split black gram, powder, sesame seeds, poppy seeds, cumin seeds. Add tamarind, garlic and grind them. Take it all into a big bowl and mix thoroughly. Tasty black chilli powder is ready to use. Heat 50ml of oil and mix in the powder.

# Powder Used in Curries

**Ingredients**

| | | | |
|---|---|---|---|
| Chilli powder | 1 kilo | Cumin seeds powder | 75 grams |
| Coriander seeds powder | 100 grams | Garlic | 75 grams |
| Fenugreek seeds powder | 25 grams | Salt (fried) | 50 grams |
| Split Bengal gram | 50 grams | Black gram | 50 grams |

**Method of preparation**

Grind all the ingredients in a mixer. Store it in a dry bottle. If used carefully (do not use wet hands or wet spoon) it can be stored up to a year. It can be added to all curries and soups.

For fries, grind chilli powder ½ kilo, fried cumin powder 100 grams and salt 100 grams. Add 4 garlic pods before adding to any curry.

# Curry Leaves Powder

**Method of preparation**

Take ½ kilo black chilly powder (nalla karam) and mix ¼ kilo powdered curry leaves in it. Curry leaves must be cleaned, dried and powdered. In the same way, coriander, mint leaves can be cleaned, dried and powdered. If mixed in black chilli powder, we get the powder we want. If it does not taste good, a bit of tamarind, salt and garlic can be mixed.

# Recipe - Rasam Powder

**Ingredients**

| | | | |
|---|---|---|---|
| Split red gram | 1 glass | Cumin seeds | ¼ glass |
| Pepper | ¼ glass | Garlic pods | ½ glass |
| Asafetida | ½ tbsp | Coriander seeds | 1 glass |
| Dried Curry leaves (powder) | ½ cup | | |

**Method of preparation:** Fry all the ingredients in ghee separately and prepare powders. Add garlic pods and grind all of them together. Do not mix much after adding garlic. It will become pulpy. Mix it lightly. Otherwise add four garlic pods whenever rasam is to be prepared. Soak lemon-sized tamarind. In a pan, saute the seasoning ingredients in ghee. Add 2 spoons of thinly chopped onion and tomato. After they are fried, pour the tamarind water. Add 1 spoon of rasam powder, salt to taste, 4 spoon of turmeric and boil. After boiling twice, add coriander before removing. It tastes good with rice.

# Fish Curry Powder

**Ingredients**

| | | | |
|---|---|---|---|
| Coriander seeds | 50 g. | Cumin | 50 g. |
| Sounf | 10 g. | Fenugreek | 50 g. |
| Dry chilli powder | 50 g. | Curry leaves | 50 g. |
| Garlic | 75 g. | Rock salt | 50 g. |
| Kasoori methi | 10 g. | Tamarind | 50 g. |
| Turmeric | 25 g. | Rice (fry till the colour changes into red) 50 g. | |

(Wherever the garlic is there peel it and grind it and fry the garlic in ghee and add to the powder)

**Preparation:** Fry all the  ingredients lightly on low flame and make powders in mixi and store in glass jar.

# Egg Curry Masala Powder

**Ingredients**

| | | | |
|---|---|---|---|
| Coriander seeds | 50 g. | Cinnamon | 25 g. |
| Black Cardamom | 25 g. | Pepper | 25 g. |
| Cloves | 25 g. | Sounf | 10 g. |
| Curry leaves | 50 g. | Turmeric | 25 g. |
| Dry Pudina powder | 75 g. | Dry Red Chilli | 75 g. |
| Cumin | 50 g. | Star Anise | 20 g. |
| Garlic | 50 g. | Rice | 50 g. |
| Black Salt | 75 g. | | |

**Method of preparation**

Fry lightly on low flame make the powders and add all the powders and store it in the glass jar.

# Biryani Masala Powder

**Ingredients**

| | | | |
|---|---|---|---|
| Black cardamom | 15 g. | Black Pepper | 25 g. |
| Bay leaf | 50 g. | Dry Mirchi | 25 g. |
| Cloves | 20 g. | Kasoori methi | 25 g. |
| Javithri | 20 g. | Star Anis | 10 g. |
| Asafotida | 10 g. | Shajeera | 10 g. |
| Cinnamon sticks | 15 g. | | |

**Method of preparation:** Fry lightly all the masala powders and store them in a jar.

# Tanduri Chicken Powder

**Ingredients**

| | | | |
|---|---|---|---|
| Coriander seed | 500 g. | Red gram (split) | 50 g. |
| Cinnamon stick | 50 g. | Cloves | 25 g. |
| Black cardamom | 25 g. | Poppy seeds | 50 g. |
| Star Ani | 25 g. | Bay Leaf | 50 g. |
| Nutmeg | 1 no. | Asafotida | 20 g. |
| Dry Mirchi Powder | 75 g. | Mustard Seeds | 25 g. |
| Rock salt | 50 g. | Cumin powder | 50 g. |
| Sount | 25 g. | Garlic | 100 g. |
| Turmeric | 25 g. | | |

**Method of preparation:** Fry all the ingredients lightly on low flame and make powders in mixi and store in glass jar.

# Chicken Masala Powder

**Ingredients**

| | | | |
|---|---|---|---|
| Coriander seeds | 500 g. | Poppy seeds | 50 g. |
| Black cardamom | 10 g. | Cinnamon | 25 g. |
| Dry Chilli Powder | 50 g. | Fenugreek | 25 g. |
| Star Ani | 25 g. | Javithri | 25 g. |
| Cloves | 25 g. | Kasuri Methi | 50 g. |
| Nutmeg | 2 nos. | Shazeera | 25 g. |
| Pepper | 50 g. | Sount | 25 g. |
| Cumin | 50 g. | Turmeric | 25 g. |
| Garlic | 75 g | Asafotida | 25 g. |
| Raw Bengal gram split | 50 g. | Rock salt | 10 g. |
| Sounp | 25 g. | Rice (fry till the colour changes into red) | |

**Method of preparation**

Take all the ingredients and fry lightly on low flame, make powders and mix all the powders, store in a glass jar.

# Meat (Mutton) Masala Powder

**Ingredients**

| | | | |
|---|---|---|---|
| Coriander seeds | 500 g. | Cloves | 25 g. |
| Cinnamon | 25 g. | Pepper | 50 g. |
| Cardamom | 25 g. | Star Ani | 25 g. |
| Poppy seeds | 75 g. | Kasoori Methi | 50 g. |
| Pudina (Mint) Dry powder | 75 g. | Cumin | 75 g. |
| Rock salt | 50 g. | Mustard | 25 g. |
| Garlic | 50 g. | Split raw Bengal gram | 25 g. |
| Rice (fry till the colour changes into red) | 75 g. | Turmeric | 25 g. |

**Method of preparation:** Fry all the ingredients lightly on low flame and make powder and store in a glass jar.

# Tea Masala Powder

| | | | | |
|---|---|---|---|---|
| **Ingredients:** | Cloves | 10 gm. | Cardamom | 3 nos. |
| | Cinnamon | 5 gm. | Nutmeg | 5 gm. |
| | Javithri | 5 gm. | Mace | 5 gm. |
| | Saunt | 5 gm. | | |

**Method of preparation:** Dry roast all on a small flame and make powders separately. Add all the powders and store in a glass jar. For one cup of a tea use a pinch of powder and the tea will taste very good. It is very good for throat also.

Non-Veg
Recipes

# Egg Curry

**Ingredients**

| | |
|---|---|
| Eggs | 4 (boiled) |
| Turmeric | ¼ tspoon |
| Onions | 2 (chopped) |
| Salt | to taste |
| Green chilli | 2 |
| Cinnamon | 1 inch piece |
| Ginger | little |
| Cardamom | |
| Garlic | 4 pods |
| Oil | 2 tbsps |
| Chilli powder | 1 tsp |

**Process of preparation**

Grind onion pieces and green chilly coarsely in mixer. Add all the other ingredients and grind again. Put a pan on stove and pour oil. Fry the ground paste. Add boiled, peeled eggs, salt chilli powder, turmeric powder. Before removing the pan, garnish with grated coriander. It tastes very good.

# Egg Sour Curry

**Ingredients**

| | |
|---|---|
| Eggs | 4 (boiled) |
| Onion | 1 (chopped) |
| Tamarind | lemon-sized |
| Oil | little |
| Green chilli | 2 (chopped) |
| Ginger garlic paste | little |
| Chilli powder | little |
| Clove | 1 |
| Turmeric powder | ¼ spoon |

**Process of preparation**

Place a thick bottomed sauce pan on stove and pour oil. Saute seasoning ingredients. Add onion, green chilli pieces, ginger garlic paste and cloves. After they are fried, add tamarind water. After it thickens, add boiled eggs and remove it. Before removing the pan, garnish with coriander. It tastes good with rice.

# Scrambled Egg

**Ingredients**

| | | | |
|---|---|---|---|
| Eggs | 4 | Turmeric powder | ¼ tsp |
| Onions | 2 (chopped) | Salt | to taste |
| Green chilly | 1 (chopped) | Oil | 2 tsps |
| Chilli powder | little | | |

**Method of preparation**

Heat oil in a pan. Fry onion and green chilly pieces. Add turmeric powder, and salt. Crack eggs sond add it. After it is fried, remove the pan. It tastes good with rice and chapatti.

# Chicken Biryani

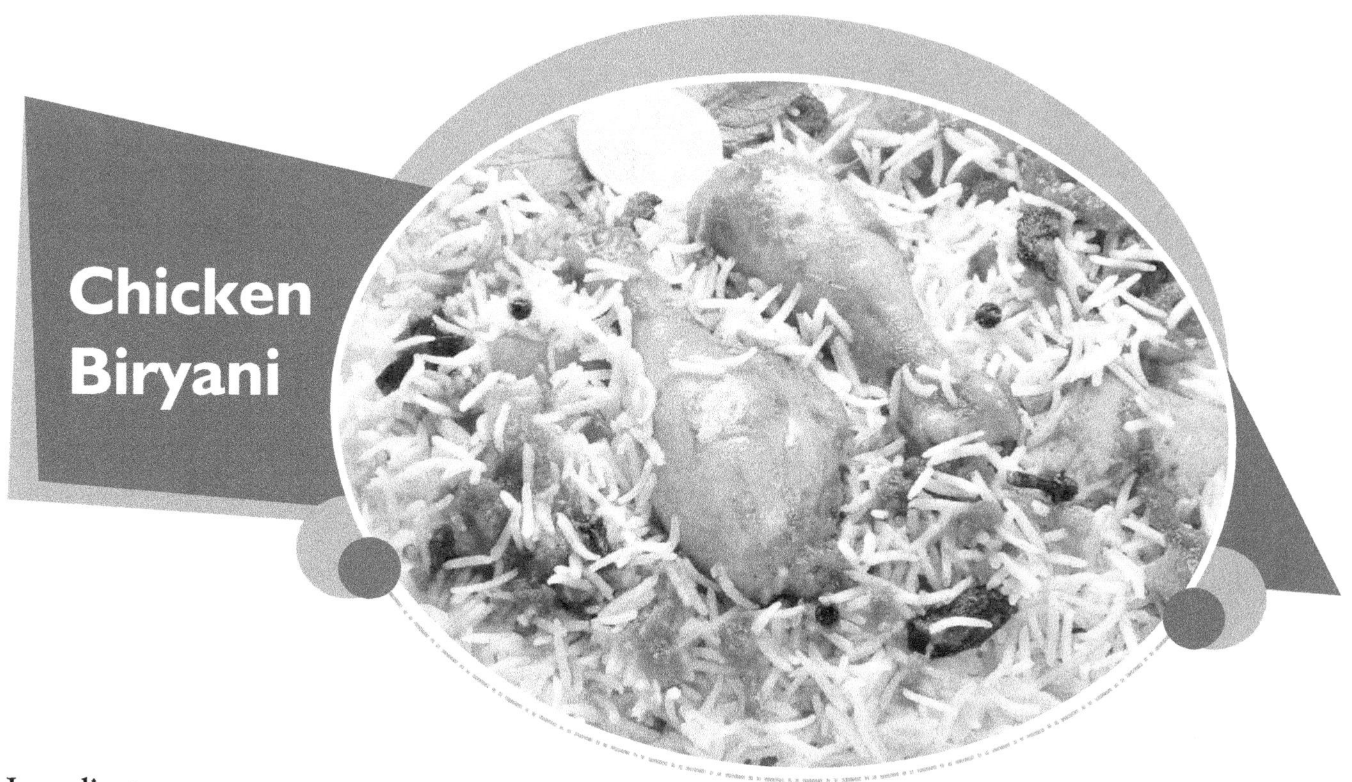

## Ingredients

| | | | |
|---|---|---|---|
| Chicken | 1 kilo | Basmati rice | 3 cups |
| Onion | 1 big (chopped) | Garlic paste | 2 tbsps |
| Ginger paste | 2 tbsps | Turmeric powder | ¼ tsp |
| Chilli powder | 1 tbsp | Salt | to taste |

| **Masala Powder** | | **Masala Paste** | |
|---|---|---|---|
| Sounf/fennel | ½ tbsp | Green chilly | |
| Poppy seeds | 2 tbsps | Coriander leaves | 2 tsps |
| Pepper | 6 nos. | Pudina/mint leaves | 1 tsp |
| Cinnamon | 1 inch | Onions | 2 (chopped) |
| Green cardamom | 3 | Oil or ghee | 1 tbsp |
| Black cardamom | 2 | Coriander chopped | |
| Cloves | 6 nos. | | |

## Method of preparation

Put a pan on the stove and pour oil or ghee. Fry onions till they turn golden brown and put them aside. Put a thick pan on stove and fry chicken pieces. Later add ginger, garlic paste, onion pieces, turmeric powder, and chilli powder and put the lid. Allow it to cook. Add masala paste and salt. Simmer down the flame and cook for 15-20 minutes. After chicken softens, add masala paste. Let it cook without much wetness. Add 3 cups of rice and mix. Add 5 cups of water, fried onion pieces, salt if necessary, and let it cook for 15-20 minutes. It can be best served 5 minutes after cooking. In other way, cook chicken pieces, salt, turmeric powder, a bit of ginger garlic paste, 1 cup of curd together. Put a pan on stove, pour oil and fry 4 cloves, a bit of cinnamon, a piece of nutmeg, mace, pineapple flower, biranji leaf, a bit of shajeera, 10 cashew nuts. Add pudina leaves, onion pieces, green chilli, coriander, ginger garlic paste. Pour 2 glasses of water for 1 glass of rice. Add salt and all the ingredients along with cooked chicken pieces. After rice is cooked, garnish it with coriander after 5 minutes. It is best served hot. If more water was used while boiling chicken, pour less water while boiling it along with rice. If everything is prepared in advance, this method will be easy.

## Ingredients

| | |
|---|---|
| Chicken (cut into pieces) | ½ kg |
| Onions | 2 nos. (sliced) |

### Spice Paste

| | |
|---|---|
| Poppy seeds (khus khus) | 2 tsp. |
| Coriander seeds | 1 tsp. |
| Dry Red Chillies | 4 nos. |
| Green Cardamom | 2 nos. |
| Cinnamon stick | 1 pc. |
| Cloves | 4 nos. |

### For gravy

| | |
|---|---|
| Ginger + Garlic paste | 3 tsps |
| Coconut extract milk | ½ cup |
| Curd 3/4 cup | |
| Salt to taste | |

### Process of preparation

Fry lightly gravy items (except red chilli), grind the roasted spices and the red chillies into a smooth paste. Blend the curd and keep aside.

Now heat the pan and put the chicken pieces in and roast both sides. Add sliced onions, ginger and garlic paste fry for few minutes, put in the spice paste, add salt to taste. Cover and cook on slow heat for 20 to 25 minutes till the chicken is tender add coconut milk cover for 2 to 3 minutes more and remove the kurma from the stove and it is ready to serve.

## Roast Chicken

### Ingredients

| | |
|---|---|
| Chicken pieces | ½ kg |
| Ginger Garlic paste | 2 tsp. |
| Pepper Powder | 2 tsp. |
| Salt | to taste |
| Oil to fry | 50 gms. |

### Process of preparation

Clean the chicken pieces, dry the chicken pieces well. Rub with salt, ginger and garlic paste and keep aside for one hour.

Heat the oil on stove, fry the chicken pieces and it is ready to serve.

## Chilli Chicken

### Ingredients

| | |
|---|---|
| Chicken (cut into medium pieces) | ½ kg |
| Oil | 50 ml. |
| Large onion | 1 (diced) |
| Spring onions | 3 tsp. (chopped) |
| Ginger | 1 tsp. (chopped) |
| Green Chillies (chopped) | 4 nos. (small) |
| Garlic cloves | 2 to 3 nos. |
| Pepper powder | 1½ tsp. |
| Soya Sauce | 2 to 3 tsp. |
| Salt | to taste |
| Kasurimethi | 1 tsp. (add to chicken) |

### Process of preparation

Marinate the chicken pieces in soya sauce and pepper for 2-3 hours. Drain the marinated well and keep it aside. Pre-heat the vessel add oil drop in the marinated chicken and roast well on both sides. Mix in the garlic, chopped ginger, green chillies and diced onions. Add a pinch of salt if required, cover and cook till the chicken is tender. Drop up the excess moisture and the marinated chicken and the chopped spring onions. Stir fry for a few minutes. Remove from the heat and change into serving bowl. Serve hot with fried rice or noodles.

# Mutton Dum Biryani

**Ingredients**

| | | | |
|---|---|---|---|
| Mutton | 250 grams | Turmeric powder | a pinch |
| Basmati rice | 250 grams | Chilli powder | 2 tsp. |
| Ginger Garlic paste | 1 tsp | Salt | to taste |
| Curd | little | Garam masala | ½ tsp |

**Process of preparation**

Cook all the ingredients except rice upto three whistles in a cooker. Wash and soak 250 grams basmati rice and cook 3/4th of it. In a pan, pour oil and fry onions. Add cinnamon, shajeera, another onion, ginger garlic paste, coriander, pudina and half of the cooked mutton. Mix them. Add half of the cooked rice and the remaining mutton. Add the remaining rice on it. Garnish it with fried onion.

# Keema Lettuce Curry

**Ingredients**

| | | | |
|---|---|---|---|
| Mutton keema | ¼ kilo | Chilly powder | 1 tsp |
| Lettuce | 2 cups (chopped) | Turmeric powder | 1 tsp |
| Ginger garlic paste | 1 tsp | Salt | to taste |
| Onions | 2 (chopped) | Oil | 3 tbsps |
| Green chillies | 2 (chopped) | Garam masala | ½ tsp |
| Garam masala powder | 1 tsp | Coriander | little |

**Method of preparation**

Wash keema. Strain water  add salt, turmeric powder, ginger garlic paste and cook till 2 whistles in a cooker. Put a pan on stove and heat oil. Add chopped onions, green chilli and fry till they turn red. Add chopped lettuce. After lettuce is cooked, add cooked keema and let them fry well. Add chilli powder, garam masala powder and cook them for 2 minutes. Garnish it with coriander before removing the pan.

# Mutton Curry

**Ingredients**

| | |
|---|---|
| Mutton | ½ kilo |
| Onions | 2 |
| Green chillies | 4 |
| Ginger garlic paste | 2 tsps |
| Oil | 2 tsp |
| Cloves | 4 nos. |
| Coriander | 2 tsps |
| Cinnamon | 2 inches |
| Salt | to taste |
| Cardamom | 2 |
| Chilly powder | 2 tsps |
| Garam masala | 1 tsp |
| Turmeric powder | ¼ tsp |
| Shajeera | a pinch |

**Process of preparation**

Cook mutton, one spoon of ginger garlic paste, salt, turmeric powder in cooker. Cut onions, green chilli into long slices and put them aside. Put a pan on stove and pour oil. Add cloves, cinnamon, shajeera, cardamom, onion, green chilli pieces, ginger garlic paste and cook. Add cooked mutton, salt, chilli powder, turmeric powder and let them cook. Cook them all for 10 minutes. Garnish it with coriander. It tastes good with rice, chapattis.

# Peas and Keema Curry

**Ingredients**

| | |
|---|---|
| Peas (boil separately) | 1 cup |
| Keema (boil separately) | ¼ kilo |
| Ginger garlic paste | 2 tbsps |
| Onions | 2 |
| Green chilli | 4 nos. |
| Oil | 2 tsps |
| Cardamom | 2 nos. |
| Curry leaves | few |
| Coriander Cloves | 4 nos. |
| <u>Masala Powder</u> (dry roast all and make them powders) | |
| Cinnamon stick | 2 inch |
| Coriander seeds | 2 tsp |
| Poppy seeds | 1 tsp |
| Cloves | 4 nos. |

**Process of preparation:** Place cooker on stove, pour oil. Add onion, green chilly pieces, ginger garlic paste and cook. After cooking keema and peas add 1/2 cup of water, salt, chilli powder, turmeric powder, masala powder and cook. After the curry thickens, garnish with coriander and remove the cooker. It tastes good with rice and chapattis. It is also good for health.

# Tawa Gost

**Ingredients**

| | | | |
|---|---|---|---|
| Mutton | 1 kilo | Jaaji bud | 1 |
| Garam masala powder | 2 tsps | <u>Garam masala spices</u> (dry roast all and make powder) | |
| Ginger garlic paste | 2 tbsps | Poppy seeds | 1 tbsp |
| Ghee | 50 grams | Coriander seeds | 1 tsp |
| Onions | 4 | Nutmeg | 1/4 piece |
| Tomatoes | 2 | Cardamom | 2 nos. |
| Chilly powder | 2 tsps | Cinnamon | 1 inch |
| Salt | to taste | Cloves | 4 nos. |
| Coriander | 1 tsp (grated) | Mace | 2 nos. |

**Method of preparation:** Clean the mutton pieces. In a pressure pan, cook mutton pieces add salt, chilli powder and after add masala powder. In a thick pan, fry mutton pieces in ghee. In another pan, add onion pieces, tomato pieces, green chilli and ginger garlic paste in ghee or oil. Add masala powder and mix. Lastly, add ground poppy seeds and grated coriander.

# Mutton Kurma

**Ingredients**

| | | | |
|---|---|---|---|
| Mutton (boneless cubed) | 500gms. | Medium Tomato | |
| Onions sliced | 2 nos. | Ginger-Garlic Paste | 1½ tsp |
| Salt | to Taste | Green Coriander | ¼ cut |

**Spice Paste**

| | | | |
|---|---|---|---|
| Cloves | 2 nos. | Cinnamon slices | 1 or 2 pcs. |
| Green cardamoms | 2 nos. | Dry Red Chillies | 4 nos. |
| Coriander seeds | 2 tsps | Oil | ½ tbsp |
| | | Curd | ½ cup |

**Process of preparation**

**Preparation for Spice Paste:** On low heat fry all the ingredients and make them into a paste.

**Preparation for Recipe :** On low heat fry the mutton cubes, add onion sliced, add the grinded paste and fry well, add tomatoes and salt to taste. Stir once or twice, cover and cook the mutton till it becomes tender. Remove the lid and garnish with coriander, ready to serve. It is very tasty with rotis, chapathis and rice.

# Mutton Khada Masala

**Ingredients**

| | | | |
|---|---|---|---|
| Boneless mutton | 1 kilo | Turmeric powder | 1/4 tsp |
| Ginger garlic paste | 3 tbsps | Chilli powder | 2 tsps |
| Curd | 1 cup | Mustard oil | 20 ml. |
| Coriander powder | 1 tbsp | Coriander | little |
| Cumin powder | 1 tsp | Salt | to taste |
| Garam masala powder | 1 tsp | | |

**Process of preparation**

Wash and chop mutton into small pieces. To the churned curd add coriander powder, cumin powder, garam masala powder, turmeric powder, salt, chilli powder, ginger garlic paste. Add mutton pieces to this mixture and let it soak for half an hour. In a thick pan, heat oil. Fry the mutton pieces little bit. Put a lid on it and cook it till it softens. Garnish it with coriander.

# Dhaniya Keema Matar (Coriander Keema Peas)

**Ingredients**

| | | | |
|---|---|---|---|
| Mutton Keema | ½ kilo | Coriander seeds powder | 3 tsp |
| Raw peas | ½ cup | Chilli powder | 2 tsp |
| Grated coriander | little | Curd | ½ cup |
| Oil | 4 sps | Salt | to taste |
| Onion | 2 (chopped) | Ghee | 1 tbsp |
| Garam masala | 1 tbsp | Turmeric powder | ¼ tsp |
| Ginger garlic paste | 2 tbsps | | |

**Method of preparation**

Chop onion into pieces. Boil peas. In a small bowl, mix coriander seeds powder, chilli powder, turmeric powder, salt, curd and put it aside. Fry onion pieces in oil. Add garam masala, ginger garlic paste and fry for some more time. Now add curd mixture and let it cook. Add keema and cook for 2 minutes. Pour enough water. Add ghee and put the lid. Boil it till the water has evaporated. Add peas and cook for some more time. Garnish with coriander and serve hot.

# Sorel Leaf with Mutton

**Ingredients**

| | | | |
|---|---|---|---|
| Mutton | ½ kg | Onions | 2 nos. (sliced) |
| Green Chillies | 4 slit | Red Chilli Powder | 1 tsp. |
| Turmeric Powder | ¼ tsp | Salt | to taste |
| Sorel leaves | 2 cups | Oil | 3 tsp. |
| Coriander leaves | ¼ cup (chopped) | Mint leaves | ¼ cup (chopped) |
| Ginger Paste | 2 tsps | Garlic Paste | 2 tsp |

**Spice Paste / Powder**

| | | | |
|---|---|---|---|
| Cumin Seeds | 1 tsp. | Cinnamon Stick | 2 inch |
| Cloves | 4 nos. | Dhania Powder | 1 tsp |
| Cinnamon stick | | | |
| Poppy Seed | 1 tsp (make it fine pasta and keep it aside) | | |

(Roast all the ingredients of cumin and coriander seeds and make powder it)

**Method of preparation**

Cook the mutton well, add ginger and garlic paste and salt, also turmeric powder. Cover and cook for 40 minutes till tender. Add one spoon of oil in a bowl and add the ginger and garlic pasta all the cooked sorel leaves, onions, mirchi powder, mint leaves and methi leaves, Spice paste and cook well after 4-5 minutes change the curry into serving bowl.

# Ridge Gourd (Beerakaaya) Shrimps Curry

**Ingredients**

| | | | |
|---|---|---|---|
| Ridge Gourd | 1/4kg | Mirchi powder | 1 tsp |
| Shrimps (peeled & cleaned) | 1/4 kg | Turmeric powder | 1/4 tsp |
| Onion (cut into pieces) | 1 no. | Salt | to taste |
| Green Chillies (cut into pieces) | 3 nos. | | |

**Process of preparation**

Peel off ridge gourd and cut into pieces. Cut into pieces onion and green chillies. Clean shrimps, cut into pieces, apply salt and turmeric to pieces. Heat oil in a pan, saute seasoning ingredients, once they splutter, add pieces of onion, green chillies, curry leaves. After for one minute, add shrimps. While cooking, put ridge gourd pieces, salt, mirchi powder, turmeric powder and cover with a lid, leave it to cook in a low flame. No additional water is required as the water content in ridge gourd and shrimps is sufficient for the recipe to cook well. This recipe tastes different without any added masala.

## Shrimp Fry

### Ingredients

| | |
|---|---|
| Shrimps (peeled and cleaned) | 1/2 kg |
| Cinnamon | 2 inch piece |
| Onions (cut into pieces) | 1 no. |
| Cardamom | 2 nos. |
| Green chillis (cut into pieces) | 3 nos. |
| Shajeera | 1 pinch |
| Mirchi powder | 1 tsp |
| Oil | 2 tsp |
| Turmeric powder | 1/4 tsp |
| Coriander leaves | few |
| Tomatoes (cut into pieces) | 4 nos. |
| Mint leaves | few |
| Ginger-garlic paste | 1 tsp |
| Garam masala | 1 tsp |
| Cloves | 2 nos. |
| Curd | 1/2 cup |

### Process of preparation

Add curd while cooking any Non-veg. item for a good taste. Curd is not necessary. While preparing curry add juice of one piece of lemon. Put Shrimps, salt, turmeric powder in a cooker and cook well up to 2 whistles. Heat oil in a pan, add cloves, patta, cardamom, shajeeera, mint leaves and saute well. Add pieces of onion, green chillis, ginger garlic paste, saute until the flavor of ginger garlic paste changes. Add tomato pieces, when half boiled, add cooked shrimp pieces to this mixture and allow it to fry well. Add garam masala while frying. Put mirchi, turmeric powders while frying. Verify the taste of salt in the mix before putting salt, as we have mixed salt while cooking shrimps. Leave the entire mixture to cook well. Garnish with coriander leaves. If you want dry fry, then do not add tomatoes. This recipe tastes good with rice, chapathi and dosa.

## Shrimp Pulao

### Ingredients

| | |
|---|---|
| Shrimps (peeled and cleaned) | 1 kg |
| Curd | 1 cup |
| Basumati Rice | 1/2 kg |
| (clean and soak in water) | |
| Cloves | 2 nos. |
| Water in the ratio | 1:2 |
| Cinnamon | 2 inch piece |
| Ginger-garlic paste | 1 tsp |
| Cardamom | 2 |
| Onions pieces | 2 cup |
| Shajeera | 1 pinch |
| Garam masala | 1 tsp |
| Coriander leaves | 1/4 cup |
| Oil | 1/4 cup |
| Mint leaves | 4 cup |
| Salt | to taste |
| Curry leaves | 4 petals |
| Turmeric powder | 1/2 tsp |

### Process of preparation

Put pieces of shrimps in a cooker, add salt, turmeric powder, curd, half ginger garlic paste and cook until two whistles are blown. Grind well coriander leaves, mint leaves few, green chillies in a mixer and keep aside. Heat oil in a pan, saute cloves, cinnamon, cardamom shajeera, cut pieces of onion, green chillies. After sautéing well, add ginger garlic paste and saute until the flavor changes. After two minutes, add soaked rice and water in the ratio 1:2, while cooking add pieces of cooked shrimps. Verify the taste of salt in the mix, as salt is already added in shrimp pieces. Put the above mixture in a cooker and while cooking stir two times in the middle so that all the ingredients are mixed properly. Do not stir many times, as shrimp may be cut into pieces. Garnish with coriander leaves. Combination of curd raitha (perugu pacchadi), chicken and mutton kurma tastes very good with this recipe. Add shrimps after cooking the rice for some time. Add garam masala (optional) while adding shrimps.

# Fish Sour Curry

**Ingredients**

| | |
|---|---|
| Fish | 1 kilo |
| (sole fish/korrameenu/rava chepa) | |
| Salt | to taste |
| Onions | 2 |
| Chilli powder | 2 tsps |
| Green chillies | 5 |
| Turmeric powder | 2 tsps |
| Ginger garlic paste | 2 tsps |
| Curry leaves | |
| Tamarind | lemon sized |
| Coriander powder | 2 tsps |
| Tomatoes | 1/4 kilo |
| Cumin powder | 1 tsp |
| Oil | 50 grams |
| Fenugreek seeds | 1/2 tsp |

**Process of preparation**

Clean the fish, cut into pieces and keep aside. Chop onion, green chillies, tomatoes into pieces and keep aside. Clean tamarind and soak in water. Apply salt, turmeric powder to cut fish pieces, clean them again and keep aside. Heat oil in a shallow bowl add fenugreek seeds, chopped onions, green chillies, curry leaves and fry. Now add coriander powder, cumin powder, tomato pieces, ginger-garlic paste. Fry these ingredients well. Add cut fish pieces, salt, mirchi powder, turmeric powder, after one minute add tamarind juice, simmer let it cook well, garnish with coriander leaves. Instead of using tamarind juice, we can use mango pieces, tamarind leaf powder. This tastes very good with any of the ingredients mentioned.

# Fish Fry

**Ingredients**

| | |
|---|---|
| Fish | 1 kilo |
| Chanduva fish is preferred | |
| (can be cooked with any fish) | |
| Thick tamarind pulp | 3 tsps |
| Ginger garlic paste | 2 tsps |
| Chilli powder | 2 tsps |
| Turmeric powder | ½ tsp |
| Salt | to taste |
| Oil | 50 grams |
| Coriander (grated) | |
| Sliced green chilli (for garnishing) | |

**Process of preparation**

Add tamarind pulp, salt, chilli powder, turmeric powder, ginger garlic paste to the fish pieces and leave it for half an hour. Put a pan on stove and heat oil. Fry the pieces. The pieces can also be deep fried if wanted. They can be shallow fried on a pan also to cut down the oil used. Put them in a dish. Garnish with coriander and green chilli pieces. It looks good and is tasty.

## Mutton Fry

**Ingredients**

| | |
|---|---|
| Mutton | 1Kg |
| Onions | 3 nos. (sliced) |
| Green Chillis | 6 nos. (slit) |
| Tomatoes | 3 nos. (grind) |
| Salt | 2 spoons (half add first) |
| Chilly Powder | 2 spoons (half add first) |
| Turmeric | ¼ spoon (half add first) |
| Oil | 2 spoons (one Spoon) |
| Mutton Masala Powder | 1 tbsp |

**Process of preparation**

Mix all ingredients with mutton pieces - half of the onions, half spoon salt, half spoon chilly powder, half spoon oil - mix well and keep on the stove. After 4,5 whistles, keep it on the stove for draining the water.

Keep the pan on the stove, pour oil (1 spoon), add ginger and garlic paste, fenugreek leaves 1 bunch, turmeric, curry leaves, tomato, spring onion 1 Bunch, after cooking for 5 minutes add mutton stir well, add onion pieces, green chillis, red chilly powder and garam masala. Let it fry for 7, 8 minutes and sauté well. Add coriander leaves and take it into serving bowl. Tasty mutton fry is ready.

## Crab Curry

**Ingredients**

| | |
|---|---|
| Crab | 1 Kg. |

(After cutting the crab, wash the pieces thrice thoroughly with ½ teaspoon salt and turmeric. Marinate with salt 1 teaspoon, chilly powder 1 teaspoon, turmeric powder 1 teaspoon. Keep it aside for one hour.)

| | |
|---|---|
| Onion (cut into 4 pcs.) | 2 nos. big size |
| Tomatoes (cut into 4 pcs.) | 3 nos. |
| Cumin | 1 teaspoon |
| Coriander | 2 teaspoons |
| Garlic | 6 pods |

(Grind all these in a mixture jar and keep it aside)

| | |
|---|---|
| Green Chillis | 4 nos. (slit) |
| Tomatoes | 2 nos. (cut into pieces) |

(Grind these two separately and keep it aside.)

**Process of preparation**

Heat oil in a pan and add ½ spoon fenugreek seeds, after 5 min add onion masala and after 3 min add green chillis and tomato paste. Fry for 2 min. on a low flame, add ginger garlic paste, curry leaves, tomato puree, sauté it. Properly fry it for 2 min. cover it and after 2 min. fry it on low flame. Add one teaspoon ghee, salt, marinated crab pieces and slowly fry. After 2 minutes add one glass of water and cook for 3 minutes, after adding the masala powder let it cook for2 mins. and remove from the stove and add coriander leaves. Take it into serving bowl.

| | |
|---|---|
| Cloves | 3 nos. |
| Cinnamon | 3" |
| Cardamom | 3 nos. |

Grind softly and add to curry before removing curry and add chopped coriander. The curry will taste very good.

Sweets

# Semolina Sweet Chapatis
## (Rava Bobbatlu)

**Ingredients**

| | |
|---|---|
| Bombay Rava | half kg |
| Coconut | 1/4 kg |
| Sugar | half kg |
| All purpose flour (maida) | half kg |
| Clarified butter (ghee) | 50g |
| Cardamom powder pieces | |

**Process of preparation**

Roast semolina (Bombay Rava) lightly and place it aside. Make single string sugar syrup and add semolina (Bombay rava) and grated to the syrup. Mix thoroughly on a low flame while pouring semolina (Bombay rava) into the sugar syrup to avoid the formation of balls. Allow the sweet mixture to cool down. Make dough of the all purpose flour (maida) with water and place it aside for an hour. Make balls of the sweet mixture and place them in the pellets of the all purpose flour (maida). Roll into chappathis and fry dough like roti on both sides with clarified butter (ghee). Relish the semolina coconut sweet roti.

# Moong Dal Rotis
## (Pesara Bobbatlu)

**Ingredients**

| | |
|---|---|
| Split (moong dal) | 1/4 kg |
| Clarified butter /ghee | 50 g |
| Sugar | 1/4 kg |
| Cardamom powder | 6 pieces |
| Peni rava | 1/4 kg |

**Process of preparation**

Clean moong dal and after soaking for an hour, grind it. Steam the soaked moong dal and powder the same Prepare a single string sugar syrup on a low flame and add the powder of moong dal. Add cardamom powder and mix it thoroughly to avoid the formation of lumps. Allow the sweet mixture to cool. Make sugar balls of it. Prepare dough of semolina peni rava and leave it aside for an hour. Take a plastic cover or a banana leaf or almond leaf and place the sweet ball in the pallet of semolina (peni rava) dough and cover the sweet ball with the dough completely. Press them gently with hand to increase it to the size of a tortilla (roti). Prepare tortilla (roti) on a pan with clarified butter (ghee). Savour the sweet tortilla hot or cold.

# Sweet Tortilla (Bobbatlu)

**Process of preparation**

This dish plays a pivotal role in the sweet dishes. They are very auspicious, tasty and the appetite. This dish tastes good with ghee when hot. Bobbatlu tastes delicious with milk.

# Rava Kesari

**Ingredients**

| | | | |
|---|---|---|---|
| Semolina (Bombay Rava) | 1 cup | Sugar | 1½ cup |
| Ghee | 1½ cup | Milk | 3 cups |
| Cashew nuts | 15 pcs. | Raisins | 10 pcs. |
| Kesari colour | 1 pinch (optional | | |

**Process of preparation:** Add two spoons of ghee in a pan to roast cashews & raisins on low flame till it turns into light colour. Remove them and keep them aside. Add two more spoons of ghee to the same pan and slightly roast rava on low flame till it turns golden brown colour. Take a pan and boil 3 cups of milk, keep adding rava to the milk on low flame and stir it till the milk absorbs the rawa. Now add sugar to the rava and it gets loose. Keep stirring it. When the mixture gets thick, add the remaining ghee and stir it without forming lumps. When the gee comes out from the sides add cashewnuts and raisins. If needed add a pinch of colour mixed in a spoon of water and transfer it into a bowl.

# Mysore Pak

**Ingredients**

| | |
|---|---|
| Bengal gram flour | 1 cup |
| Sugar | 2 cups |
| Ghee | 2½ cups |

**Process of preparation**

Dry roast gram flour till you get nice aroma for 5 minutes. Add ½ cup of warm melted ghee to the flour and mix thoroughly without lumps. Take 2 cups of sugar in a bowl, add ½ cup of water to it and place it on the stove for 10 minutes till it gets string consistency. Add flour to the syrup and keep stirring continuously without lumps till it thickness. Simultaneously heat 2 cups of ghee in a bowl, when it gets too hot start adding ghee in small quantity to the flour start absorbing the ghee. When the mixture starts releasing ghee from the sides, transform this immediately into a greased pan and set the top by slightly pressing. After 10 minutes cut it with greased knife into pieces. Reverse the pan and tap it to remove the pieces.

# Split Chick Peas Sweet Rotis
## (Senaga Pappu Bobbatlu)

**Ingredients**

| | |
|---|---|
| Split chick peas (channa dal) | 1/2 kg |
| Oil | 150 g |
| Grated Jaggery | 1/2 kg |
| Cardamom (powdered) | 2 pieces |
| All purpose flour (maida) | 1/4 kg |

**Process of preparation:** Clean and cook split chick peas with two cups of water. Remove excess water from the cooked channa dal vessel and allow it to cool. Grind boiled split chick pea (channa dal) along with grated jaggery and cardamom powder. Prepare all purpose flour (maida) dough with water and oil and leave it for an hour. Place sweet balls in the pallets of dough. Press them gently with hand to increase it to the size of a roti. Prepare roti on a pan with clarified butter (ghee) or oil. Savour the sweet rotis hot with clarified butter.

# Sweet Rice Pudding
## (Teepi Payasam)

**Ingredients**

| | |
|---|---|
| Rice | Two cups |
| Cashew nuts | half a cup |
| Milk | Six cups |
| Clarified butter | 2 tsp |
| Grated Jaggery | half kilo |
| Raisins | a few |
| Cardamom (powdered) | 2 pieces |

**Process of preparation:** Boil milk with a little water and then add cleaned rice into it. Add grated jaggery to the cooked rice followed by roasted (with clarified butter) cashew nuts, raisins, cardamom powder. Pudding could be made with sugar or jaggery. Sugar, jaggery syrup or sugar/jaggery could be added as per convenience. Savour the simple sweet rice pudding.

# Vermicelli Pudding
## (Semiya Payasam)

**Ingredients**

| | |
|---|---|
| Vermicelli | 1/4 kilo |
| Cashew nuts | ten |
| Milk | half litre |
| Raisins (kismis) | ten |
| Sugar | 500 gm |
| Clarified butter | 2 tsp |
| Cardamom powder | six pieces |

**Process of preparation:** Fry vermicelli in 1 spoon of ghee till it is light brown. Boil milk with a little water and then add vermicelli to it. Add sugar to the cooked vermicelli followed by roasted (with clarified butter) cashew nuts, raisins and cardamom powder. Add sago (saggu biyyam or sabudana) if required for taste. (sago takes a lot of time to boil. So, semi boil it before adding to the vermicelli.) Savour this simple vermicelli pudding.

# Doughnuts

**Ingredients**

| | | | |
|---|---|---|---|
| Semolina (Rava) | 100g | Sugar | 50 g |
| Milk | 100 ml | Fennel seeds (saunf) | 10g |
| All purpose flour (Maida) | 50g | Cardamom powder | a pinch |
| Wheat flour | 50 g | Oil or clarified butter | 2 tsp |

**Process of preparation:** Soak semolina for twenty minutes in hot milk. Make slurry by mixing all purpose flour and wheat flour thoroughly with water and leave it for ten minutes. Mix soaked semolina to the slurry. Make single strand sugar syrup and add fennel seeds, and cardamom powder to it. Deep fry balls of the slurry and put them in the sugar syrup. Enjoy sweet doughnuts.

## Coconut Sweets
## (Kobbari Boorelu)

**Ingredients**

| | |
|---|---|
| Grated coconut | one |
| Rice | one kg |

(soak it four hours prior to the preparation of the dish and grind it to powder)

| | |
|---|---|
| Grated Jaggery | one kg |

**Process of preparation**

Make jaggery syrup with water in a big vessel on a low flame. Add grated coconut powder to the boiling jaggery syrup. Once the coconut powder is boiled, turn off the flame. Add rice flour to the jaggery and coconut syrup while stirring slowly and continuously to avoid formation of lumps. Mix the mixture thoroughly. See to it that the mixture is not very hard nor very loose (let it be medium) to be able to form balls of the mixture for deep fry. Boil the oil in a deep pan. Prepare balls of mixture and make flat on wet cloth or a leaf. Deep fry the flat sweets. They get fried easily. Carefully lift the fried balls from oil. Place them on a tissue paper or a plate. Savour the delicious coconut jaggery sweet on any festive or get together function.

## Complete Jaggery Sweets
## (Purnam Boorelu)

**Ingredients**

| | |
|---|---|
| Channa dal (split bengal gram) | half kg |
| Moong dal (split green gram) | one cup |
| (soak it for two hours and make paste) | |
| Rice | half cup |
| (soak it for two hours and make paste) | |
| Grated jaggery | half kg |
| Cardamom powder of | 4 pieces |
| Oil | 1/4 kg |

**Process of preparation**

Cook Channa dal in a cooker up to 2 whistles. Remove excess water from the channa dal container. Make a paste of cooked channa dal along with grated jaggery. Cook this paste on a low flame and add cardamom powder. Now grind this paste completely. Prepare balls of channa dal and jaggery and dip them in the dough of rice and black gram dal. Deep fry these balls of the mixture on a low flame. Carefully remove the fried sweet balls on a tissue paper to a plate. This sweet is considered to be auspicious and offered during poojas. Savour the complete and delicious sweets on all the festivals. All purpose flour (maida) could be used in place of moong dal. Soak rice and black gram in water and grind well make the batter to dip the balls.

## Plain Jaggery Sweets (Bellam Boorelu)

**Ingredients**

| | |
|---|---|
| Rice | half kg (soak for three hours dry in shade & make flour) |
| Grated Jaggery | half kg |
| Oil | 1/4 kg |

**Process of preparation:** Prepare one string jaggery syrup by placing a vessel on low flame with one glass of water. Add rice flour to the jaggery syrup and stir continuously to avoid the formation of lumps. Prepare balls of mixture and make flat on wet cloth or a leaf. Deep fry the flat sweets. Carefully remove the fried sweet balls onto a tissue paper placed on a plate. Savour the simple and delicious sweets.

# Carrot Pudding (Carrot Payasam)

**Ingredients**

| | |
|---|---|
| Milk | half litre |
| Sugar | 50g |
| Cardamom powder | 1/4 spoon |
| Almonds | 15g |
| Grated carrot | two cups |
| Clarified butter (ghee) | 50g |
| Cardamom pieces powder | two |
| Raisin (kismis) | 15g |
| Cashew nuts | 15g |

**Process of preparation:** Roast grated carrot till the smell is lost then add cashew nuts and raisins and place it aside. Boil milk by adding a cup water to it. Add the roasted grated carrot. Add sugar and cardamom powder to the boiled milk for 2 mins. Garnish pudding with almond soaked and pealed nuts and raisins. Savour the delicious pudding.

# Carrot Porridge
## (Gajar or Carrot Halwa)

**Ingredients**

| | |
|---|---|
| High fat milk | 500g |
| Almonds (badam) | 10 |
| Sugar | 60g |
| Cashew nuts | 10 |
| Grated carrot | 250g |
| Clarified butter | 2 tsps |
| Condensed milk (Koya) | 150g |

**Process of preparation:** Heat the toned milk in a thick deep vessel. Add grated carrot and boil the milk for three minutes. Boil carrot milk for twenty minutes or till it is being thickened. Stir a few times. Add sugar when it is almost thickened. Add condensed milk, clarified butter and any essence and mix it thoroughly. Boil it for three minutes. Remove the contents in a plate. Garnish it with almonds and cashew nuts. Savour the delicious carrot porridge.

# Carrot Dense Milk Confectionery (Carrot Burfi)

**Ingredients**

| | |
|---|---|
| Milk  100g | |
| Almonds | 15g |
| Grated carrot | 250g |
| Clarified butter (ghee) | 30g |
| Cardamom pieces powder | five |
| Pistachios (pista) | 30g |
| Cashew nuts | 30g |

**Process of preparation**

Boil milk with grated carrot. Add sugar to the boiling milk till the sugar is separated from the boiling vessel. Add clarified butter cardamom powder and allow it to cool. Apply clarified butter on a plate and then pour the boiled milk mixture on the plate. Garnish the mixture with cashew nuts and pistachios. Relish the Carrot dense milk confectionery (carrot burfi).

# Caramel Custard

**Ingredients**

| | |
|---|---|
| Milk | half litre |
| Eggs | 3 |
| Sugar | 5 tsps |
| Vanilla essence | 2 tsps |

**Process of preparation**

To prepare caramel, place a thick vessel on stove and pour five table spoons sugar and sprinkle water on it. Take sugar syrup into another bowl. Mix the vanilla essence with the contents of broken eggs (yolk) and stir this mixture thoroughly. Boil milk with sugar. Add vanilla mixed yolk to the dissolved sugar milk and blend it thoroughly. Pour the boiled milk mixture on the caramel lining. Cover it with a grease proof paper and steam cook it. After thirty minutes the custard is set. Allow it to cool & store it in the refrigerator.

## Globules Sweet Balls
### (Boondi Laddo)

**Ingredients**

| | |
|---|---|
| Bengal gram flour (besan) | four cups |
| Soaked and peeled almonds | a few |
| Rice flour | one cup |
| Raisins | a few |
| Sugar | five cups |
| Baking powder | ½ tsp. |
| Cashew nuts | 50g |
| Oil | half kilo |
| Cardamom pieces | 10 |
| Edible Camphor | a little |
| One Special Globule Sieve (bundi Laddo Garita) | |

**Process of preparation**

Mix chickpea flour (besan), rice flour, baking powder with water to form a dough of runny consistency. Deep fry the mixture by pouring it onto the special sieve with another small deep sieve and place aside. Prepare a single strand sugar syrup with water and add cashew nuts, fried raisins, edible camphor, finely cut almonds and finally the fried flour globules. Mix them thoroughly and make medium sized spheres (laddo) of it, sugar syrup is crucial in this dish.

## Sweet Semolina Balls
### (Rava Laddu)

**Ingredients**

| | |
|---|---|
| Semolina (bombay rava) | 1/2 kilo |
| Cardamom powder | 5 pieces |
| Sugar | 1 kilo |
| Clarified butter (ghee) | 1 tsp |
| Cashew nuts | 25g |
| Hot milk | 4 kilo |

**Process of preparation**

Shallow fry semolina (bombay rava) with clarified butter (ghee) till the aroma is felt and place it aside. Shallow roast cashew nuts with clarified butter (ghee) till the colour changes to golden colour. Boil milk and place it aside. Prepare a powder of sugar and place it aside. Mix semolina (bombay rava), sugar powder, cashew nuts, cardamom powder along with hot milk. Make spheres (laddoo) of the mixture. This tasty sweet can be made in thirty minutes.

## Condensed Milk Sweet (Palhari Basundi)

Preparation Time 20 Mins & Boil for 45 Mins

**Ingredients**

| | | | |
|---|---|---|---|
| Milk | 1½ litre | Fruit pulp | one cup |
| Sugar | 6 tsps | Cardamom powder | a pinch |

**Process of preparation**

Boil milk on a low flame till it becomes half. Stir the boiling milk. Add fruit pulp and cardamom powder and allow it to cool. Savour Condensed milk sweet (palhari basundi)

## Badusha

### Ingredients

| | |
|---|---|
| Water | 4 glasses (pour into a vessel) |
| Sugar | 6 glasses (make into syrup) |

(Need not make it thick. Only Boil it for 2 minutes without bubbles. Set the syrup in another bowl.)

| | |
|---|---|
| Cardamom Powder | One spoon |
| Maida | One Kg. |
| Curd | 10 tb spoons |

### Process of preparation

Take maida in a bowl, add curd, Half spoon Baking Powder and adding water slowly. Make the Maida into dough like chapathi and make small balls and make the balls into small Badusha shape in middle with your finger press the Badusha and other side also press it and keep aside. After making all badushas like this, light the stove, keep a pan and pour refined sunflower oil (one Kg), heat the oil and drop the Badushas, when they are coming up, remove them and keep aside. Light the stove again, drop the Badushas in the oil once again and remove them after they become golden brown. Drop the Badushas into cooled sugar syrup. Make all the Badushahs like this. Now tasty Badushas are ready to eat. Add 3 spoons of ghee to syrup. Keep the dough for one hour before making the balls. Knead the dough nicely.

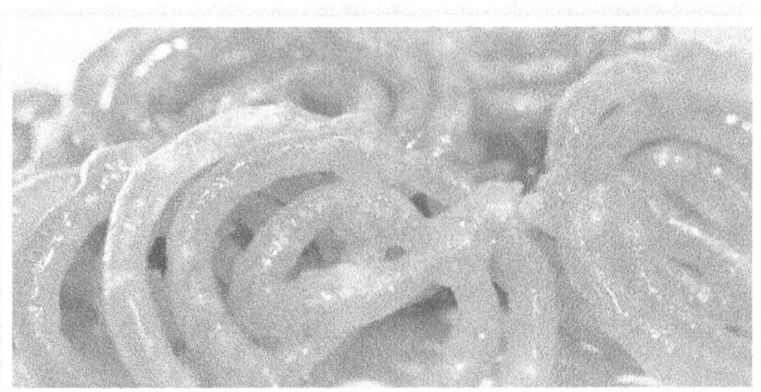

## Jilebi

### Process of preparation

Take two glasses sugar and add one glass of water to make syrup. In the syrup add ½ spoon cardamom powder, after syrup is ready, add one spoon ghee also.

Prior to the day you are making Jilebi, prepare dough.

Take 4 glasses maida, add 1½ glass curd (sour) and add some water. Keep the dough for 10 to 12 hours. Next day take the dough and add ¼ spoon baking powder and make the dough like dosa batter.

Make the syrup and let it cool. Put a pan on stove, pour 750 grams refined sun flower oil. Take a cloth in between the cloth make a hole, and stitch the hole. Take the Batter in the cloth, hold the cloth four sides and squeeze the batter in oil making round Jilebis, after the Jilebis get brown color take out the Jilebis and put them in syrup. Just press the Jilebis in syrup lightly and take them from syrup after 2 minutes. Repeat all the Batter in same method. Tasty Jilebis are ready. Same way you can make Jaggery Jilebis also.

## Sreekhand

### Ingredients

| | | | |
|---|---|---|---|
| Curd | 2kgs. | Milk | 8 glasses (to set curd) |

**Process of preparation:** Tie the set curd in a cloth. If you want to make in the morning prior to the day night take the cloth and put the curd in it, and tie it high. And keep the plate with holes and keep another plate under the holes plate. After 5 to 6 hours water will stop coming out from the curd. For 2 ltr. curd, we get 600grams cake. Add 600 grams sugar for the cake. Make sugar as powder, add sugar powder in the cake and add ½ spoon nut meg powder, cinnamon powder ½ spoon saffron powder a pinch, pistachio pieces. This will be very tasty with Puri, Chapathi and Pulka, for Dosa and idly also it will be very tasty.

Tiffins

# Idli

**Ingredients**

| | |
|---|---|
| Para boiled rice | 4 cups |
| Split black gram | ¾ cup |
| Salt | to taste |

Soak para boiled rice and split black gram separately for 4 to 5 hours. Adding little water, grind the soaked gram into smooth batter. Similarly grind the rice. Mix the two batters and add a pinch of salt. Cover the batter and keep the batter in a warm place to ferment for 10 to 12 hours, over night will do.

**Process of preparation**

Add a little water ½ cup to fermented batter, it will get a thick pouring consistency, grease the mould of Idli stand and pour a ladleful of batter into each of them, stack 3 to 4 racks and steam them for approximately for 7-8 minutes. Take the stand out, cool it for 3 minutes before removing the Idlis. Serve hot with chutney or sambar.

# Veg. Upma

**Ingredients**

| | | | |
|---|---|---|---|
| Samolin (Raw / sooji) | 2 cups | Large Potato | 1 (diced) |
| Carrot large | 1 (diced) | Shelled Peas | ½ cup |
| French Beans | 4 to 6 (chopped) | Onions | 2 nos. (chopped) |
| Green Chillies | 2 to 3 nos. (split) | Ginger | 1 tsp. (chopped) |
| Water | 4 cups | Salt | to taste |

**Seasoning:**

| | | | |
|---|---|---|---|
| Black gram split | 1 tsp. | Mustard Seeds | 1 tsp. |
| Curry Leaves | 5 to 6 | Coriander Leaves | 2 tsp. |
| Red Chillies | 2 nos. | Ghee / Oil | 1 tsp. |
| Lemon Juice (optional) | 1no. | | |

**Process of preparation**

Pre-heat the high level vessel on slow heat. Put the oil or ghee and drop onions. Stir for few minutes till light pink. Add all vegetables dripping wet cover and cook till the vegetables get soft. Pour in the water and add salt, simmer till the water begins to bubble. Mix the Samolina (rava) in, stir well, cover and cook for few minutes. Remove from the heat and add the seasoning.

For the seasoning pre-heat the vessel, add ghee or oil, put red chillies, split black gram and crushed ground nuts fry on low heat till golden brown. Add the mustard seeds and curry leaves, once mustard seeds splatter, pour the seasoning over the semolina mixture. Stir and sprinkle with coriander leaves. Keep covered for few minutes before serving. Serve hot with a chutney of your choice.

## Masala Dosa

**Ingredients**

| | | | |
|---|---|---|---|
| Para boiled Rice | 2 cups | Split Black gram | ½ cup |
| Salt | to taste | | |

**Filling**

| | | | |
|---|---|---|---|
| Large potatoes cooked | 2 nos. (diced) | Medium Onion | 1 no. (sliced) |
| Chopped Ginger | ½ tsp. | Green Chillies | 2 nos. (chopped) |
| Mustard Seeds | few | Turmeric Powder | ¼ spoon |
| Split Black gram | 1 tsp. | Curry leaves | 6 to 8 |
| Chopped Coriander Leaves | 1 tsp. | Oil | 2 tsp. |
| Salt | to taste | | |

**Process of preparation**

For Dosa Batter soak the rice and split black gram separately in sufficient water for 4-5 hours. Drain it and keep aside. In a mixer grinder grind the gram into a smooth, light and fluffy paste by adding water slowly, and grind the rice also. Mix both the pastes together adding ½ table spoon salt. Cover and keep it form fermentation for 10 to 12 hours. Overnight is best. Add approx. ½ - 1 cup of water to the batter to make dosas. The remaining batter should be stored in an air tight container for later use. On frying pan make dosa with one table spoon of batter apply oil before putting dosa.

**for filling:**

Gently mash the potatoes. Pre-heat the vessel on low heat. Add oil to the split black gram and mustard seeds. Once the seeds splatter add the onions, ginger, green chillies and curry leaves. On low heat fry the onions like light pink. Mix in the cooked potatoes, turmeric powder and salt. Add ½ cup of water and simmer for few minutes. Sprinkle coriander leaves and remove from the heat, let it cool and divide into 5 portions, grease a skillet with 2 table spoons of oil and pre-heat and remove the lid and skilled around to spread oil evenly. Pour a ladle full of dosa batter in the centre. Spread the batter in quick motion circularly to form dosa. Dizzle all around with little oil, cover and cook on low heat the dosa becomes little brown on one side. Flip over and cook other side. Turn it over place a portion of the filling in the centre of the dosa and fold it over. Remove it and place it on a serving plate. Absorb excess oil from the skilled with a tissue cloth. Prepare the remaining dosas following the same method without adding any oil and serve hot with coconut chutney.

## Mysore Bonda

**Process of preparation**

Take 3 glasses maida, ½ teaspoon baking powder, cumin 1 teaspoon, salt add all and keep it whole night (approx. 12 hrs.). Next morning take the dough, knead it nicely. Consistent should be thick only not loose. Take a pan and keep it on the stove pour oil and heat it. Make small balls and put in the oil. After half fry remove the balls and keep them side. Repeat the same process. After half fry, put the first balls also in the oil. After changing the colour take the bondas with chutneys like ginger chutney and coconut chutney it tastes good. If you like you can add onion pieces, green chilly pieces, ginger pieces, cumin powder with all these it will taste good.

## Ivy gourd instant chutney

**Ingredients**

| | |
|---|---|
| Ivy gourd | ½ kg. |
| Lime juice | 5 limes |
| Chilly powder + fenugreek + mustard seeds (fry lightly make it powder) | 5 tsps. |
| Garlic paste | big size 2 nos. crushed |
| Oil | 150 gms. |

**Process of preparation**

Keep the pan on stove add 150 gms. Oil, heat the oil and add seasonals –mustard seeds, cumin seeds and asofoeteda ¼ tsp, curry leaves, crushed garlic, dry red chillis 2 pieces - fry them on slow flame and them in ivy gourd pieces. Add salt, chilly powder, all the powders, turmeric ¼ teaspoon. Mix oil after it gets cool and lime juice, chutney is ready. Keep in a glass jar.

# Chutnies

## Green Chilly Chutney

**Ingredients**

| | |
|---|---|
| Green chilly | ¼ kg |
| Garlic | 10 pods |
| Soaked Tamarind | 100g |
| Red chilly powder | 1 tsp |
| Grated coconut | One cup |
| Split black gram | 1 tsp |
| Oil | 1 tsp |
| Split bengal gram | 1 tsp |
| Coriander seeds | 2 tsp |
| Salt | a pinch |
| Cumin | 1 tsp |
| Turmeric powder | 1 tsp |

**Process of preparation:** Shallow fry green chillies for a while till the colour has changed and place it aside. Roast lightly coriander, split black gram, split bengal gram, cumin and make a powder of this mix and keep it aside. Grind the fried green chillies along with tamarind, garlic pods, add the powder mix and salt. Relish the mouth watering spicy delicacy with plain red gram and plain rice.

## Coconut Chutney
### (for Dosas and Idli)

**Ingredients**

| | |
|---|---|
| Grated coconut | One cup |
| Coriander leaves | a little |
| Green chilly | 6 nos. |
| Cumin powder | 1/2 tsp |
| Tamarind | a little |
| Oil | 1 tsp |
| Salt | a pinch |
| Curry leaves | 4 sprigs |

Ingredients of seasoning (all mix) 1 tsp

**Process of preparation**

Shallow fry green chillies and allow it to cool. Grind fried green chillies, coconut, tamarind, and cumin powder. Shallow frying radients for seasoning and add to the ground chutney with curry leaves and salt. This chutney is delicious with idli and dosa.

## Carrot Chutney

**Ingredients**

| | | | |
|---|---|---|---|
| Carrots (Pieces) | 2cups | Salt | to taste |
| Cumin | 1 tsp | Green Chillies | 5 Nos. |
| Cooking oil | 1 tsp | Lime Juice | little bit |
| Garlic | 2-3 pods | Curry leaves | A few sprigs |
| Cumin & Mustard seeds | As required | Coriander leaves | A few twigs |

**Process of preparation**

Chop Carrots and Green Chillies into small pieces and set aside. Place a frying pan on lighted stove. Pour oil in it and after the oil is heated sufficiently, add Cumin & Mustard seeds along with Curry leaves for seasoning purpose. Grind Carrot pieces, Cumin, Garlic (peel off its skin and crush) and salt and add this paste to the seasoned oil. Now, add chopped Coriander, and Lime juice before removing from stove.

## Coconut Chutney with Green Chilly

**Ingredients**

| | |
|---|---|
| Green chilly | ¼ kg |
| Grated coconut | One |
| Curry leaves | 4 |
| Green chilly | 10-15 |
| Garlic | 6 pods |
| Tamarind | lemon sized |
| Seasoning ingredients | 1 tsp |
| Salt | a pinch |
| Coriander | 1 tsp |
| Cumin powder | 1 tsp |
| Fenugreek seeds | 1 tsp |
| Oil | 1 tsp |
| Coriander leaves | |

**Process of preparation**

Shallow fry green chillies and allow it to cool. Shallow fry and make a powder of coriander, cumin, fenugreek seeds. Grind fried green chillies, add garlic and salt followed by grated coconut and tamarind. Now add powder mix along with curry leaves. This chutney tastes good with or without seasoning.

## Coconut Chutney with Dry Red Chilly

**Ingredients**

| | |
|---|---|
| Grated coconut | One |
| Curry leaves | 4 |
| Dry red chilly | 10 |
| Garlic | 6 pods |
| Tamarind | Lemon sized |
| Coriander | 1/2 tsp |
| Salt | a pinch |
| Fenugreek | 1 tsp |
| Cumin powder | 1 tsp |
| Coriander leaves | |

**Process of preparation:** Shallow fry dry red chilly, fenugreek, cumin, and coriander and place it aside. Grind all of the above along with tamarind, garlic, salt and grated coconut. Add curry leaves, and coriander leaves and take it in a separate bowl. This chutney tastes good without seasoning.

## Red Ripe Chilly Chutney (Pandu Mirapa Pachadi)

**Ingredients**

| | | | |
|---|---|---|---|
| Riped Red chillis | 1 kg | Fenugreek seeds powder | 15 gms |
| Tamarind | 1/4 kg | Ginger | 2 inches |
| Salt | 100 gms | Jaggery | 2 inches |
| Garlic pods | 1/4 kg | Turmeric powder | 100 gms |

**Process of preparation**

Clean the ripe red chillies and dry them, remove the stalk from the chillies. Grind the red chillies. Place red chilly paste in a jar by mixing salt and turmeric powder. Place tamarind in the jar along with the red chilly paste. Grind once again after 4 days. Allow it to marinate for nearly a week. Add garlic pods and fenugreek powder to this paste. This does not require seasoning. If interested, you can season the red chilly chutney. Take some red chilly chutney grind it once again, add curd, cumin seeds powder and season it. This tastes good with Idli and Dosa.

# Pickles

## & Vadiyalu

# Lemon Pickle

**Ingredients**

| | | | |
|---|---|---|---|
| Lemons | 100 | Salt | 300 gms |
| Mirchi powder | 300 gms | Turmeric powder | 15 gms |
| Garlic pods | 150 gms | | |
| Fenugreek powder | 50 gms (dry roast fenugreek seeds to red colour and grind to powder) | | |
| Green chillies | 200 gms (slice them into two halves vertically) | | |
| Ginger | 200 gms (cut into long pieces) | | |
| Bitter gourd | 4 kgs (cut into long pieces) | | |

**Process of preparation**

Put lemon pieces, green chillies pieces, ginger and bitter gourd pieces, salt and turmeric powder in a glass jar for 4 days. Remove the pieces from jar on the fourth day and dry them in the hot sun. Add mirchi powder, fenugreek seeds powder, crushed garlic pods to lemon pieces in the jar. If required squeeze some lemons in the jar for lemon juice. This does not require seasoning. If required, you can add salt and mirchi powder, despite using the measurements.

# Mango Pickle (for One Year)

**Ingredients**

| | |
|---|---|
| Raw Mango Pieces | 8 cups |
| Dry Chilli Powder | 1 cup |
| Mustard Seed Powder | 1 cup (raw) |
| Fenugreek seed Powder | 300 g. (lightly roasted) |
| Salt | 1 cup |
| Raw Fenugreek seeds | 50 g. |
| Raw Chana (full) | 25 g. (bengal gram full) |
| Turmeric Powder | 3 tsps |
| Garlic (Peeled & cleaned) | 1 kg. |
| Garlic paste | ½ kg. |
| Gingelly oil | 2 kg. |

**Process of preparation**

First make pieces and dip the pieces in ½ kg. gingelly oil and set aside. Add dry red chilli powder, fenugreek powder, mustard powder, fenugreek seeds, full Bengal gram seeds, garlic paste, garlic pods, salt, turmeric powder, and add all the ingredients to mango pieces, add another ½ kg. oil and set aside. 3rd day open the mango pieces jar and see if all the ingredients are well added and if needed pour some more oil. This pickle can be used for one year if salt and oil are sufficient

# Dry Mango Pickle

**Ingredients**

| | |
|---|---|
| Peeled Mango Pieces (raw mango should be little long) | 8 cups |
| Mustard Powder | 100 g. (raw) |
| Fenugreek seed Powder (roasted) | 50 g. |
| Salt | 1 cup |
| Garlic | 1 kg. |
| Dry Red Chilli Powder | 1 cup |
| Turmeric powder | 25 g. |
| Gingelly oil | 1 kg. |

**Process of preparation:** In mango pieces add half of the salt and turmeric powder, keep it aside for 3 days. After 3 days squeeze the mango pieces and keep them in the sun. After in squeezed juice remain salt and other ingredients all of them put in mango pieces, after sauting all properly, take a pan keep it on the lighted stove, pour oil and season it and take it into a glass jar, once taste the salt and store the pickle. It will be very tasty. Dry roast lightly mustard and fenugreek seeds and powder it.

# Kenaf Leaves Pickle
## (without Chilli Powder)

**Ingredients**

| | |
|---|---|
| Kenaf leaves | 1 kg. |
| Tamarind | 100 g. |
| Salt | 100 or 125 g. |
| Oil | 100 g. |

<u>Note:</u> Dry roast fenugreek powder it and add to kenaf leaves.

**Process of preparation:** Clean kenaf leaves. You should clean it for two times. Clean the leaves, take out the hard ends. Keep a pan on stove add 100g. oil, kenaf leaves, add salt to it fry the kenaf leaves till the leaves become soft and water should absorb. Take the tamarind and wash in hot water. Take turmeric and tamarind mix in kenaf fried leaves. Keep it in a jar. Whenever you want, fry green chillies and mix with kenaf leaves, add garlic pods, curry leaves, cumin seeds grind all together and season the pickle. This you can use for one year.

# Ginger Pickle

**Ingredients**

| | |
|---|---|
| Ginger (peer of its skin) | 1 kg. (make small pieces) |
| (cut into small pieces and fry them in oil) | |
| Tamarind | 1 kg. |
| Dry mirchi powder | 350 g. |
| Fried fenugreek powder | 50 g. |
| Jaggery | 1 kg. |
| Gingelly oil | 500 g. |
| Garlic | 250 g. |
| Sugar | 1 kg. |
| Turmeric | 25 g. |
| Seasoning | |

**Process of preparation:** Put a pan on stove and fry the ginger pieces. Put tamarind in hot water and cook it. After cooking the tamarind add all the ingredients grind properly. After season the pickle store it in grass jar. Because of adding the sugar it will be good and does not change colour.

# Kenaf Pickle
## (long Lasting)

**Ingredients**

| | |
|---|---|
| Kenaf leaves | 1 kg. |
| Fried Red Mirchi Powder | 100 g. |
| Tamarind | 100 g. |
| Salt | 125 g. |
| Fried Fenugreek powder | 75 g. |
| Mustard powder | 50 g. |
| Gingelly oil | 500 g. |
| Garlic | 300 g. |
| Seasoning | |

**Process of preparation**

Wash kenaf leaves properly strain it, after it is dry put a pan on stove pour 25 grams oil, fry lightly on low flame till it is soft. When it is hot, grind turmeric and other ingredients all together and season the pickle and store the pickle in glass jar. This is also very tasty pickle. This pickle can be used for one year if salt and oil are sufficient

# Tomato Pickle

**Ingredients**

| | |
|---|---|
| Tomatoes (slightly riped) | 1 kg. |
| Tamarind | 200 g. |
| Salt | 200 g. |
| Fried Fenugreek powder | 50 g. |
| Gingelly oil | 250 g. |
| Garlic | 150 g. |
| Dry chilli powder | 250 g. |

**Process of preparation**

Wash tomatoes neatly and dry the tomatoes with a cloth, cut the tomatoes and add half of the salt in pieces add turmeric powder also. Keep the tomato pieces in a jar. Third day squeeze the tomato pieces and you will get the juice out of it. Third day keep tamarind in this juice. After the tamarind gets soft, dry mirchi powder, remaining salt, fenugreek powder, garlic all together grind the pickle and add tomato pieces in the pickle, and season it. This tomato pickle is very tasty and you will enjoy it. If you season the pickle whenever you want, it will be good and fresh

# Garlic Pickle (Vuragaya)

**Ingredients**

| | | | |
|---|---|---|---|
| Garlic | 1 kg. (not applying oil) | Tamarind | 150 g. |
| Fried Fenugreek powder | 50 g. + Mustard powder 25 g. | Dry chilli powder | 100 g. |
| Turmeric | 2 tsps | Lime Juice | 5 nos. limes |

**Process of preparation:** Before you make tamarind pulp using a pan on the lighted stove, after making pulp, take garlic, mix chilli powder, fenugreek powder, mustard powder, mix all in tamarind pulp season the pickle. Same day when you make garlic ready you have to finish the pickle same day.

# Onion Pickle

**Ingredients**

| | | | |
|---|---|---|---|
| Onions | 100 gms. (sambar onions) | Venigar | soak till 4 hours |
| Salt | to taste | Turmeric | ¼ tsp. |
| Fenugreek powder | | Oil | 50 gms. |
| Mustard seed powder | (Fry all lightly and powder them) | | |
| Tamarind (juice) | lemon sized | Green chilly | 6 nos. (cut in to 2 pcs.) |
| Garlic | 100 gms. | Asafoeteda | ¼ spoon |

**Process of preparation:** Take onions and soak in venigar till 4 hours. Mix all ingredients in tamarind pulp. Before you make tamarind pulp using a pan on the lighted stove, after making pulp, take garlic, mix chilli powder, fenugreek powder, mustard powder, mix all in tamarind pulp season the pickle. Same day when you make garlic ready you have to finish the pickle same day.

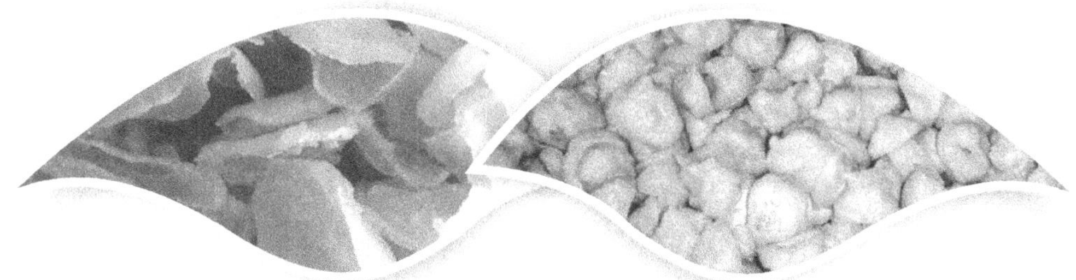

# Rice Flour Vadiyalu

**Ingredients**

| | |
|---|---|
| Rice flour | 2 cups |
| Salt | to taste |
| Water | 4 cups |
| Cumin seeds | 2 tsps |
| Green Chilli | 8 |
| Gingelly/sesame seeds (nuvvulu) | 2 tsps |

**Process of preparation:**

In a thick vessel boil 2 cups of water. Add rice flour to the other two cups of water and mix without lumps. Add this to the boiling water and stir well without lumps. After the flour is cooked, add a paste made of green chilly, salt, cumin, gingelly seeds. After it cools down, pour it into the pretzel mould (jantikala gottam) and press it in required size on a cloth. After it dries, put them in a box without breaking. Whenever you want you can roast them in oil and eat.

# Green gram Vadiyalu

**Ingredients**

| | |
|---|---|
| Split green gram | 1 kilo |
| Green chilli | 50 grams |
| Cumin seed | 4 cups |
| Coriander (chopped) | 2 cups |
| Asafetida | 1/2 tsp |
| Curry leaves (chopped) | 4 cups |

**Process of preparation**

Soak moong dal. After 4 hours, grind it along with green chilli. Add salt, cumin, asafetida, coriander, curry leaves grate and pour it in the shape of small wadas on a cloth. It should be kept in same size as urad wada. But moong is not as durable as urad. So, put it as wada before it breaks. Otherwise grind only small portions. It tastes good with onions, cooked as a curry.

# Beans Vadiyalu

**Ingredients**

| | |
|---|---|
| Beans | 1/2 kilo |
| Turmeric | 1/2 tsp |
| Salt | to taste |

**Process of preparation**

Clean the beans and remove the fibre on both sides. Put beans, salt, turmeric in a cooker and cook till two whistles. Strain the beans and dry them. They taste good as snacks in the evening when fried. They also taste good with sambar, dal.

# Mango Vadiyalu

**Ingredients**

| | |
|---|---|
| Mangoes | 10 |
| Salt | to taste |
| Turmeric | 1 tsp |

**Process of preparation:** Peel the raw mangoes and cut them into long, thin pieces. Add salt, turmeric and let it marinate for 3 days. Dry it on the third day. Put in a box carefully. They taste good with sambar and dal.

# Vadiyalu (Dry Snacks)

**Ingredients**

Oil    100 gms

**Process of preparation**

Pre-heat Tawa pour oil and put 4-5 dry snacks and after light brown colour take them out and can be used with rice-sambar and rasam.

# Dry Ash Gourd Snacks

**Ingredients**

| | |
|---|---|
| Ash gourd | 1 no. |
| Split black gram | 1 kg. |
| Salt | to taste |
| Cumin Powder | |
| Green Chillies | 5 nos. |

**Process of preparation:** Cut ash gourd into small pieces. For one night, keep the pieces under a heavy object, next day drain the water, keep it aside. In mixer grinder make split black gram as a paste, add ash gourd, salt, green chilli paste. Take a cloth and keep this like small balls smoothly press them, by evening take them from the cloth. Next day also keep them in sun, after drying store them in a jar. Deep fry 10 min. it will be very tasty in rice with sambar and rasam.

■ All varieties of vadiyalu (vadas) you have to fry (deep) them in oil

# Split Black Gram Vadiyalu

**Ingredients**

| | |
|---|---|
| Split black gram | 1 cup |
| Salt | to taste |
| Green Chillies | 2 to 3 |
| Curry Leaves | |
| Coriander Leaves | |

**Process of preparation:** Soak Black gram for 4 hours, drain the gram and make paste with chillies and salt. Add curry leaves and coriander into paste, dry them in the sun on wet cloth put them in small balls, after drying properly. Keep them in a jar whenever you want fry them in oil, it tastes good.

# Sago Vadiyalu

**Ingredients**

| | |
|---|---|
| Sago | 4 cups |
| Salt | to taste |
| Water | 16 cups (4 cups for 1 cup sago) |
| Gingelly/sesame seeds | one cup |
| Cumin | 1/4 cup |
| Green chilli | 8 nos. |

**Process of preparation:** Put water in sago and cook in a cooker till three whistles. It should be cooked till looks like sago has melted. Add cumin, salt, sesame seeds and sliced green chilli. After it cools down, pour it on a dried, wet thin cloth with a spoon in small circles. After two days, peel it and dry for few more days before transferring it to a box.

- Boiled water of leafy vegetables and cabbage could be used to prepare dough for fritters(pakodi). It is tasty and is good for health.
- Mix two tea spoons of all purpose flour to yolk of the eggs for smooth omelettes.
- If a curry is salty, add cream of the milk to decrease the saltiness.
- To decrease the cooking time of onions, add a little sugar.
- Add wheat semolina (sooji rava) to rectify sweet tortilla (bobbatlu).
- Add a piece of jaggery to store clarified butter (ghee) for long time.
- Add turmeric powder to seasoning before adding it to lemon rice or tamarind rice. It gives nice colour to the dish.
- Add a glass of sugar syrup to pulao to retain the colour and taste.
- Add black pepper powder to mango juice to increase vitality and to increase sight.
- Drink garlic, tomato juice for instant energy.
- Beetroot juice gives instant energy. Experts advise that by drinking a glass every day, one can avoid medication.
- Sesame til contains magnesium, calcium and copper. Add it to dishes to strengthen bones and joints.
- Shake soybean sauce well to let it flow easily without sticking to the bottle.
- Add pieces of beetroot to tomato soup to increase the colour and taste.
- Add a spoon of sugar to boil green peas quickly.
- While making samosa, add a few drops of lemon juice to the dough to increase the crispiness.
- To grate coconuts easily sprinkle a few drops of water on it and place it in refrigerator.
- Add two spoons of semolina (Bombay rava) and all purpose flour (maida) to the dough to enhance the taste of poori.
- Do not place a lid while cooking leafy vegetables. It would decolourise them.
- Place a lid with holes on boiled milk to increase the formation of cream.
- To avoid having split milk during summer, add two uncut (vadlu) rice grains.
- Store garlic in a polythene bag overnight in a refrigerator to peel the pods easily.
- To decrease the bitterness of bitter gourd, soak them in water used to clean rice for an hour.
- Use lemon juice and hot water to remove greasy stains on cooking platform/gas stove.
- Add a dry red chilly to decrease the time of preparing curd.
- Push a little salt in the hole to fix the screw more tightly.
- Use beetroot daily to decrease the level of cholesterol.
- Add two drops of oil and store them in air tight containers to decrease the dryness of mint leaves.
- To increase the shine of silver ware clean them with mustard powder.

- Add a cup of milk and a bit of lukewarm water to the dough to savour softened chapatti
- Add four pieces of raw mango to bitter gourd curry to decrease the bitterness.
- To have a glossy skin use fenugreek leaves at least thrice a week in meals.
- Basella alba (bacchali aaku) is tasty. It decreases thirst and also decreases gastric trouble (jathara deepti)
- Soak banana pieces in water with turmeric powder before frying to chips, to stop the chips from blackening.
- The stains on the mirror can be removed by cleaning with vinegar. Mirrors will shine.
- Clean frying pan which has curry stuck to the bottom by soaking in salt water for an hour.
- Apply lemon and sugar to the dry palms, to have smooth palms in a few days.
- Add 2 or 3 coconut pieces to sour curd.
- Keep lemon leaves in book shelves to get rid off insects.
- Add a cup of milk to the chapatti or poori dough to get softened dough and thus tortilla(chapathi).
- Apply coconut oil to lemon and store in fridge for longer duration.
- Heat the knife to cut onions, to avoid tears in eyes.
- Add two or three potato pieces to curry which has more salt, potato sucks the excess salt in the curry.
- Head ache due to summer heat can be reduced by drinking lemon and ginger mixed in lukewarm water.
- Remove hard stains in cooking vessels, use soda bicarbonate, salt and sprinkle water. All the stains can be removed.
- Overcome burning sensation in the stomach by drinking milk shake prepared with banana.
- Put orange peels in oven and heat the oven to remove bad odour in the oven.
- Maintain freshness of fruits by keeping them separately and not in covers in refrigerator.
- Old Turkish towels can be used as door mats, as they suck the water.
- Drink hot water during rainy season to avoid infectious diseases.
- When drenched in rain, take head bath with hot water and wipe with dry towel.
- Apply milk mixed with semolina (rava), besan flour to remove the dead skin.
- Apply a mix of lemon juice, almond oil and a spoon of honey to the marks on the face, which will fade in due course.
- Apply rose water with keera juice and radish juice to the skin exposed to sun.
- Apply paste of five almonds, one spoon of milk and three drops of lemon juice to dry skinfor better results.
- Massage the paste of cream of milk, basil leaves, lavender oil for bad odour of skin.
- Sprinkle turmeric powder on imitation jewellery and keep for 3 to 4 days to keep the shine intact.
- Add 1 or 2 spoons of lemon juice while cooking mushrooms for taste.

- Hang a paper immersed in kerosene near light to keep away insects during rainy season.
- Apply tomato juice, curd, basil leaves juice each one spoon to remove the sun tan on the face.
- It is advisable to drink water rather than cool drinks when on tours during holidays.
- Cook six gooseberries in a cup of milk, remove the seeds, make into a paste and apply to head, to reduce the hair fall. It makes the face fresh during summer without making itoily.
- Apply salt to the vessel to prepare the dough of chapathi, so that the dough does not stick to the vessel.
- Apply potato piece or onion piece to the pan while preparing dosas, so that the batter does not stick to the pan.
- Add fenugreek seeds to papad, so that papad is intact.
- Food cooked in iron vessels is good for health. This gives additional iron required for the body. Vegetables cooked in these vessels take more time to cook thus absorb the iron.
- Sour curd can be put in the curry leaf plant, so that the leaves get good flavour.
- Add few drops of lemon juice to ladies finger curry, to get dried curry.
- Add 4 or 5 drops of vinegar to the glass jar before storing the chutneys or pickles. Vinegar prevents fungus.
- Cut bananas and brinjals with steel knife to prevent discoloration.
- Apply tender coconut water for six months to remove scars.
- Add turmeric powder to cover used to store green chillies to retain freshness.
- Add salt to dried red chillies while frying to reduce the harsh flavour while frying.

## TIPS ON SPICES

The spice cabinet is important part of the Indian Kitchen. Buying, storing and using of spices is an art. To store the spices at homes buy whole spices do not go for powdered spices. Most spices are easy to crush and can be used for cooking before freshly grounded spices are richer in aroma and flavor.

Turmeric and Chilli hold their flavor and are normally available in the powdered form. Do not stock different spices in one container even if they are packed.

**Using Spices**

Spices have strong aroma and flavor and should be used in small quantities for best result. Always add spices and powder at the start of the cooking process. It is not wise to use extra spices at the end of the cooking process. This will give a raw flavor to cooked meal.

Always buy spices from a recognized shop.

**Sources from Vegetables:** Carrots, Green Leafy Vegetables.
**Sources from Animals:** Liver, Milk, Egg Yolk, Butter, Cottage Cheese (Paneer).

Cod Liver Oil, Egg Yolk. 

 Nuts, Seeds, Oils, Egg Yolk.

Whole grain cereals, wheat flour, bran whole pulses, egg yolk, liver. 

 Milk, Curd, whey, meat, liver, kidney, heart, leafy vegetables, yeast.

Chicken, meat, fish, liver, potato, peanuts, whole pulses and green leafy vegetables. 

 Orange, sweet lime, guava, pineapple, potato, sweet potato, tomato, green leafy vegetables.

# SOME IMPORTANT MINERALS

| | |
|---|---|
| **Calcium** | Milk and milk products like cottage cheese (Paneer), cheese, curd, etc, and whole pulses. |
| **Iron** | Green leafy vegetables, whole grain cereals, pulses dried fruits, liver, lean meat etc. |
| **Magnesium** | Grain products, milk, meat, poultry, potato, spinach, soya beans etc. |
| **Iodine** | Salt, water, fish. |
| **Fluorine** | Black tea, salt, water, fish, etc. |

One should not take salt more than 15-20 grams per day. Too much salt causes high Blood Pressure, calcium disorders, deregulates mineral balance.

Foods are classified into Groups based on their nutrient content. They are (a) cereals & millets, (b) Pulses, (c) Nuts & Oil seeds, (d) Vegetables & Fruits, (e) Milk & Milk products, (f) Eggs, (g) Meat, Poultry, Fish & Sea foods (h) Fats & oils, (i) Sugar, jaggery & other sweets items, (j) spices & condiments

(a)  **Cereals & Millets:** In general category, the large food grains like – rice, wheat, maize and their processed products (flakes, puffed / popped) are included. In millets category small grains like – Bajra (peal millet), Sorghum, Ragi (finger millet) and other minor millets like (Arika, Ooda, Sama, etc.) are covered.

(b)  **Pulses (Whole dhals):** In this category come redgram, greengram, bengalgram, blackgram, white chana (Kabooli), Corn peas, housegram, dry peas, dry beans, rajmah, dhals and roasted ones.

(c)  **Nuts & Oil Seeds:** Coconut (both fresh & dry), gram nuts, sesame (til), almonds, pista nuts, walnuts, pumpkin seeds, melon seeds, neiger seeds, sunflower seeds are covered under this group.

(d)  **Vegetables:** Classified as three categories.

    i.  **Green-leafy vegetables:** All types of leafy vegetables like spinach, amaranthus, fenugreek, chekurmani, gogu, cabbage, etc.

    ii.  **Other Vegetables:** Gourds, pumpkin, cucumber, beans, bread double beans, bitter gourd, peas, brinjals, little gourd, ladies finger, filed beans, capsicum, cauliflower, broccoli, drumsticks, raw banana, banana flower, raddish, green tomato, tender jack, fruits, mushrooms (fungi), etc.

    iii.  **Roots & Tubers:** Yarn, potato, carrot, calocasia, beetroot etc, onions, sweet potato (yellow & white).

(e)  **Fruits:** Citrus fruits (lime, sweet lime, orange, grapes), melons (musk melon, water melon), Sweet fruits (mango, sapota, jackfruit, papaya), Pineapple, grapes (blue, black, green), Kiwi, dragon, apple, guava, cashew apple, apricot, cherries, peaches, pluma, dates, pomegranate, figs, berries, stemberry, raspberry, gooseberry, cram berry, etc.

(f)  **Milk & Milk Products:** Cow milk, buffalo milk, toned milk, low fat milk, high fat milk, butter milk, curd (yogurt), milk powders (skim milk, whole milk), milk shakes, flavoured milks, basundi, rabri, cheese, khoa, paneer, flavoured (yogurts) shrikand, cream, ice creams, kulfi, casein powder.

(g)  **Eggs & Egg Products:** Poultry eggs, country eggs, duck eggs, egg products (albumin, whole egg powder), boiled eggs, omlete, cakes & pastry items, egg mage, etc.

(h)  **Meat, Poultry, Fish & Sea foods:** Goat meat, lamb meat, organ meat, pork, poultry & country chicken, nuggets, minced meat, cutlets, cheese & nuts, different types of fish (fresh water & salt water), fillete shrimps (large & small, fresh water & salt water), crabs, oysters, etc.

(i)  **Oils & Fats:** Extracted oils – Til (sesame), ground nut, coconut, miger seed, sunflower, safflower, refined oils, rice bran oil, cosmoil, mustard, olive, palm oil, butter, ghee, margarine, etc.

(j)  **Sugar, Honey & Glucose:** Sugarcane juice, honey, sugar cubes, cane sugar, palm sugar, jaggery (powder & blocks), brown sugar, corn syrup, maple syrup, sugar syrup, beet sugar, sugar candies, sugar cubes, etc.

(k)  **Spices & Condiments:** Chillies (Spicy red fresh & dry), chilli powder, ginger, pepper, cloves, azoin, garlic, turmeric, fennel,  nutmeg, mustard seeds, cumin, japatri (mace), berry leaves, asafetida, cinnamon, fenugreek, etc.

# Nutrients in different foods / groups

| No. | Foods / food groups / snack items | Nutrients present |
|---|---|---|
| i. | **Cereals:** Rice & products, wheat & products, maize & products, oats & products, barley & products | Carbohydrates, proteins, fat in small quantity, β-vitamins, Fibre, soluble starches, minerals in small amounts. |
| | **Millets:** Jowar & Products, Bajra & Products, Ragi & Products | Fibre, Carbohydrates, protein, β-vitamins, calcium, iron, low in fat |
| | **Minor Millets:** Kodo, Arika, Sama, Ooda, Quinoa | High in fibre, low in fat, moderate protein, β-vitamins & minerals small amounts |
| ii. | **Pulses:** Roasted dhals / puffed dhal powders | High in protein, carbohydrates, low in fat (except soya beans), good in β-vitamins & iron |
| iii. | **Nuts & Oil Seeds** | High in protein, fat, β-vitamins, high in fibre, calcium & iron, essential fatty acids |
| iv. | **Green leafy vegetables** (all types) | Attractive & other components (colour pigments, flavor, roughage, indigestion, pro vitamin A (β-carotene), calcium, iron, vitamin-K. |
| v. | **Other Vegetables** | Minerals, vitamins, indigestible fibre, antioxidant |
| vi. | Roots & Tubers | Soluble starches, pro vitamin-A (β-carotene), vitamin-C, some fibre – all vegetables are anti-oxidants. |
| vii. | **Fruits & Fruit products** (Protective foods) | Attractive colour compound, attractive flavor compound, vitamin-C, pro vitamin-A (β-carotene), fibre citrus & titrate components, enzymes, pectic substance. |
| viii. | **Milk & Milk products** (Protective foods) | Protein, small quantities of sugar (lactose), fat, calcium, low in fibre, β-vitamins, vitamin-D |
| | **Cow milk** | Low fat |
| | **Buffalo milk** | High fat |
| | **Cheese / Paneer** | High proteins |
| | **Rasagolla** (with sugar), **gulab-jamoon, butter & ghee** | Energy (calories), proteins, carbohydrates, fat, flavor components |

| No. | Foods / food groups / snack items | Nutrients present |
|---|---|---|
| ix. | **Eggs & their products** (highly protective food item) | High and very good quality protein, low in carbohydrates, rich in β-vitamins, iron, very high β-12 complex and phosphorus |
| x. | **Meat, Poultry & Sea foods** | High in protein, high in β-vitamin |
| | **Sea fish (most types), shrimp & crabs** | Moderate to high fat, omega-3 fatty acids, rich in fat |
| xi. | **Fats & Oils :** Butter & Ghee | Natural good fats, no carbohydrates, no proteins, good in vitamin-A & vitamin-D |
| | **Refined vegetable oils** | Good in essential fatty acids |
| | **Enriched oils** | High in vitamin-A, D, E; high smoke temperatures |
| xii. | **Sugar, Jaggery, Honey & Syrups** | High in carbohydrates, high in energy (calorie), low in fat, low in protein, flavor components |
| xiii. | **Spices & Condiments :** Chillies, pepper, onion, nutmeg, turmeric, all spice, bay leaf, mint, garlic, ginger, saffron, vanilla | Contain colour flavor components, minerals in small quantity, vitamins in small amounts, also contain antibacterial, antifungal antiviral, antiinflammatory, stimulate salivation amounts of gastric, enzyme production. Add variety and taste to food. To some extent aid in digestion &control sugar levels in blood. |

The foods eaten raw, cooked or processed have different taste in original form or with added ingredients. The inherently present (or) added ingredients influence the taste sensations of the person.

(a) salt, (b) sweet, (c) sour, (d) hot (or) spice, (e) bitter and (f) astringent

**(a) Salt** : Rock salt/sea salt are used to flavor food. They do not provide energy to the body. Some vegetables have inherent salt / sodium content. Therefore added salt should be of minimum amount. Pickles generally have high amount of salt to protect from spoilage. High salt intakes beyond 5g a day may increase blood pressure.

**(b) Sweet** : Jaggery, cane sugar, sugar syrups, fruit juices with added sugar or beetroot, carrot, sweet potato, bakery products, sweet eats are all sweets and sweet items give more energy (calories), small amount of sugar intake is ideal and more is bad for health.

**(c) Sour/Acid** : Citrus fruits – lime, sweet lime, grape fruits, grapes and their juices, berry fruits and their products, kokum fruit (dry), tamarind and the leaves green, unripe mango and mango powder (amchur), pineapple, kiwi, amla, goose berry, tomato, citric acid (salt) are sour to taste. In small amounts sour is well tolerated.

Sourness or acid ingredient is needed in pickling, tomato sauce or ketchup prep, certain types of soups, curry preparations. Sourness is required to suppress the growth of some types of bacteria.

| | | | |
|---|---|---|---|
| (d) | **Hot / Spices** | : | Chillies (fresh / dry), pepper, cloves, cardamom, azoin, ginger contribute to hot/spicy taste. Minimal amount of spice should be used to flavour foods, otherwise they may irritate stomach or gastric tract. |
| (e) | **Bitter** | : | Bitter gourd, caramel, green tea, Coffee, cocoa, chocolate over boiled tea beverage, orange peel, Lemon peel are bitter to taste. Certain gourd vegetables other than bitter gourd are poisonous, bitterness in moderation is required to keep away the intestinal parasites. |
| (f) | **Astringent** | : | Grapes, blue berries, cran berries, coffee, cocoa, black & green tea, goose berry, wood apple, wines, apple, apple juice, olives, guava, persimmon fruit are astringent in taste. |

The taste perception varies from individual to individual and according to age, gender, place of living, climate / seasons (ritus), one needs to initially choose the foods and the type of preparation to be healthy.

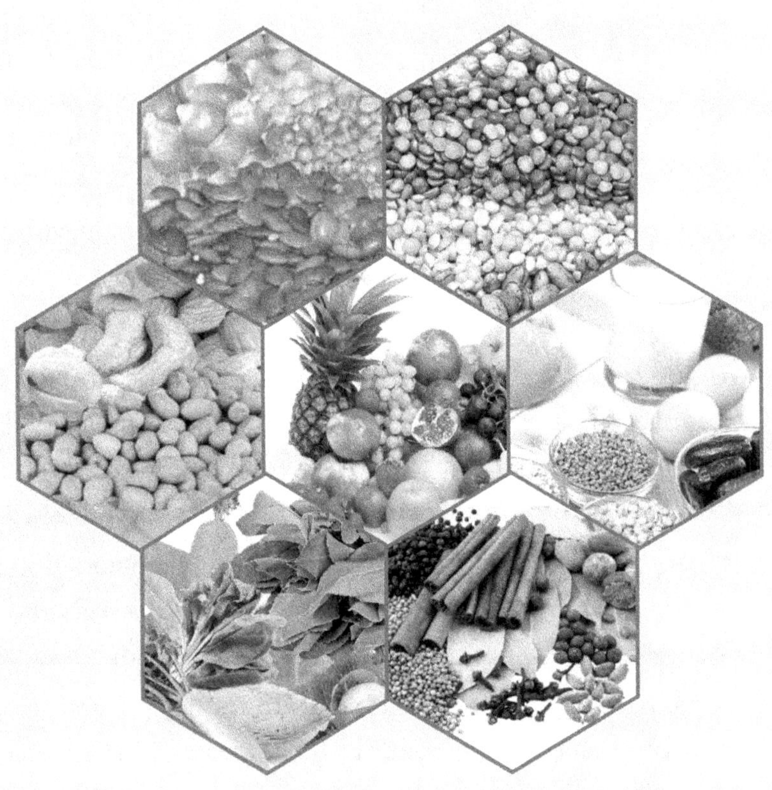

# RITUS / SEASONS IN INDIA

It was classified in the past that there are six Ritus or seasons according to climatic contribution and or temperature. They are as follows :

(a) Hemant Ritu (Pre-winter), (b) Shishir Ritu (Shita), (c) Vasant Ritu (spring), (d) Grishma Ritu (summer), (e) Varsha Ritu (Monsoon), (f) Sharad Ritu (Autumn).

To maintain good health and to protect body from heat and cold it is advisable to consume foods that are grown and amountable during the Ritus / seasons. Generally people consume food available and grown during the seasons but a judicial combination of foods intake is good to take care of changed climates. But irrespective of the season the intake of all types of vegetables, greens and fruits is essential to get adequate quantities of minerals and vitamins.

| Ritu / season | Food to be eaten | Foods to be reduced / avoided |
| --- | --- | --- |
| 1. **Hemant** (prementar / colder) (Nov 15 – Jan 14) | Heat producing food items | Very hot and spicy foods |
| 2. **Shishir Ritu** (winter / colder) (Jan 15 – March 14) | Heat producing food items | Very hot and spicy food, oily foods |
| 3. **Vasant Ritu** (spring) (March 15 – May 14) | More of protective foods – fruits, vegetables, millet, preparations – porridges | Consumption of sweet and sour foods. |
| 4. **Grishma Ritu** (summer) (May 15 – July 14) (Dry and hot) | More of liquid foods, cold beverages, butter milk, milk shakes, fruit juices, millet porridges, barley water, coconut water | Too hot and spicy food preparations, oily foods, deep fried items, pickles etc. |
| 5. **Varsha Ritu** (monsoon) (July 15 – Sept 14) | All types of foods – energy rich foods, vegetables, fruits, cow milk & milk products, ghee, goose berries, honey, jaggery, triphala, dates etc. | Citrus fruits in large amounts |
| 6. **Sharad Ritu** (autumn) (Sept 15 – Nov 14) | Light and easily digestive foods, foods which help maintain body temperature. All fruits, ghee, coconut, cow milk, gourd vegetables, green leafy vegetables, etc. | Heat causing foods, pickles, processed foods |